KAIRS
LETTERS

KAIRS
LETTERS

love letters to
believers behind bars

Michael Mann

TATE PUBLISHING
AND ENTERPRISES, LLC

Published by Tate Publishing & Enterprises, LLC
127 E. Trade Center Terrace | Mustang, Oklahoma 73064 USA
1.888.361.9473 | www.tatepublishing.com

Tate Publishing is committed to excellence in the publishing industry. The company reflects the philosophy established by the founders, based on Psalm 68:11,
"The Lord gave the word and great was the company of those who published it."

Book design copyright © 2011 by Tate Publishing, LLC. All rights reserved.
Cover design by Kristen Verser
Interior design by Kate Stearman

Published in the United States of America

ISBN: 978-1-61346-572-1
1. Religion / Christian Ministry / General   2. Religion / Christian Life / General
11.09.09

Passages quoted from the Holy Bible are taken from the New International Version (NIV) unless they have been designated differently. My own paraphrases are presented as such without quotation marks but endnoted so readers can find the references. I am a lover and student of the Bible, not a scholar or preacher. I do not pretend to have the best or most correct interpretation of God's Word but have chosen to use his words as a means of encouragement for you, beloved reader.

ACKNOWLEDGMENTS

First and foremost to God, the Father of our Lord Jesus Christ, and to his Son, and to the Holy Spirit without which neither you nor I nor this writing would be. Next, to Mosaic Fellowship, Kairos Prison Ministry International, Inc., and the Pine Lodge Corrections Center for Women for providing the purpose and original recipients of these letters. To family and close friends who read parts of the manuscript and either gave encouragement or refrained from discouraging me. To my friend in the Lord, David Preuss, for asking hard questions about doctrine, resulting in a more thoughtful and respectful exposition and some personal ah-ha moments. To Cheryl Schenk for mature help drafting the study questions. To my pastor, John Repsold, for his part in forming my life in Christ and for help with harder passages. To our pastoral intern, Luke McKinzie, for his questions about my religious past and the resulting essays that influenced this project as well. To Tate Publishing, for believing in the value of the project and for providing a positive first experience in publishing. To the photographers and owners of photos who gave permission for me to use their work. To those yet unknown who will pass the letters on to their friends and loved ones. To the staff and supporters of KSPO-FM radio and the American Christian Network for the excellent Bible teachers I have listened to nearly every day for the last dozen years. You will never know how much you have contributed to my recovery from another life. Much that I write here I learned listening to Bob Davis, Steve Winnery, Chuck Missler, David Hocking, Alistair Begg, Adrian Rodgers, J. Vernon McGee, and others on your radio network. Finally, to all my beloved who still belong to the cult from which I fled into the arms of Jesus alone for salvation and comfort. Without them, I would have little reason to write about the grace of God.

To each of you I give my heartfelt thanks.

TABLE OF CONTENTS

INTRODUCTION

Kairos Letters began as a series of four letters of faith and encouragement written for a retreat held in November of 2009 by Kairos Prison Ministry International at the Pine Lodge Corrections Center for Women in Medical Lake, Washington. Volunteers from local churches provided letters of support, plates of cookies, and posters of encouragement for the twenty-four women who signed up, and trained volunteers went into the prison for four days to conduct the retreat. When the announcement was made in my church, I felt a strong prompting to write letters. During each day of the retreat, one of the letters was given to an inmate.

The study I did of the gardens in the Bible for these letters blessed me so powerfully that I prayed to the Lord that they would be disseminated to many other women in prisons. Within about a month of the retreat, Pine Lodge became a local headline news story, as word got out that the governor had decided to close it down and move the women who were there to other facilities around the state. I don't know who got the original handwritten letters, but the story made me believe that the Lord heard my prayer.

After this, I began editing the drafts of the letters I kept and thinking about how to include images of some of the world's great gardens. While working on this, I heard a sermon on the radio that brought to my mind a garden from the Bible that I left out of the original letters, so I added a fifth letter on the garden tomb. I also wrote the final letter to share my personal witness of the resurrected Lord and suggestions for application.

Kairos is a Greek word for "time," which does not mean the ordinary flow or passage of time but rather a moment in time in which there is a crossroads, a decision, a window of opportunity that changes what follows. In each of the gardens in these letters, God takes hold of a special moment in time to demonstrate his amazing love for us in an amazing way. The original idea came a few years ago when I did a Bible study on the word *paradise*. The Greek word *paradeisos* comes from *pairidaeza*, a word from the Kurdish region of old Persia for a park. The prefix *para-* suggests that it is enclosed and protected as by a wall. In medieval Europe, it was popular to make a garden area in front of the entrance to a church and to surround it with a high wall and gate. This entrance area was called "the paradise."

As I have thought about the different gardens in the Bible, I have come to realize that paradises come in different sizes and shapes and we sometimes find them in unexpected places. Prison also has a high wall, a locked gate, and powerful guards. Perhaps there is some sense in which we can view a correctional facility as a paradise, an enclosed place where the Lord can plant a garden within our hearts. This is my prayer for you.

These letters are intimate and personal. I hope you will read them as you would read love letters written by your dear friend in the Lord who is unable to come to you personally. I realize that this study has some value for all believers, but from start to finish, I know that I have been writing to women inmates specifically. I have felt the Spirit of the Lord helping me—his great compassion for and desire to reach the women who will read this. I have enjoyed him so much during this project that I feel some reluctance to bring it to conclusion. I don't know where it will end up, but I am trusting in the Lord to use it in some way to be a blessing to you, his beloved.

PHOTO BY LEE SNIDER/PHOTO IMAGES

LETTER ONE

The Garden of Eden

My dear friend in Jesus,

When I heard that you would be doing a special retreat this week, I earnestly desired to be one of those chosen to write letters of encouragement and faith. I have been married and divorced twice and have three adult daughters, one adult son who is mentally retarded, and four grandchildren: two girls and two boys. I live with my life's losses. I was in a cult for twenty-five years and when I left it, my wife, children, and former community considered me dead or worse. I remarried but lost my second wife of ten years after a woman accused me of an act I did not commit that resulted in my professional livelihood being stripped from me. I am still on probation and have had to find a new way to make a living with a record as a potential threat to the public. The real perpetrator was never discovered. I just happened to be in the right place at the right time to become the bearer of another man's shame.

I say the *right* place, because now I realize how much God has done for me by taking away everything that made me proud of myself and my own accomplishments. The injustice I experienced was a blessing from God, who has given me a new heart and a new life in which I have pride in Jesus's goodness and his accomplishments instead of my own. I am so grateful he came not just for "people" but for me personally. How I love him for bearing my sins and shame! I was compelled to do it, but he didn't have to. Out of a love I can't understand, he volunteered.[1] This same love is now in my heart, so I want to show his love to you by taking time to write these letters.

I decided I would write each of these letters about one of the gardens found in the Bible. The garden I'm writing about today was not like any other garden in the world because God himself planted it to make a home for Adam and Eve. Nobody even knows what the world was like back then. Scientists tell us the oceans were probably shallow and warm and there was lush vegetation even in the far north and far south. It never rained in those days until the flood of Noah came.[2] Adam and Eve were naked and thought nothing of it. It was warm and pleasant for them. Eden was where the first marriage between a man and woman took place.[3] The Lord provided everything for them and, based on Genesis 3:8, we surmise that they walked and talked with him "in the cool of the day" every day. The Bible calls Eden "the garden of God"[4] but never calls it *Paradise*. That name is reserved for the place where the redeemed will be after they die.[5]

Paradise literally means an enclosure without a roof, a private garden with a wall. In the old world, gardens were not just places to grow flowers or food. They were private retreats created for enjoying peace and meditation alone or for intimacy with a loved one, a protected place where love might grow without any other distractions. Only a lord—a landowner with a considerable fortune—could afford the expense of having one. A garden of some magnitude might be found next to a castle or mansion with a high wall for privacy; a fountain of fresh water for watering the plants; every kind of fruit-bearing tree and perfume-producing herb or flower inside; and hedges, nooks, and lovely places to walk or sit and rest from the cares of life. Unlike these gardens, Eden did not have a wall; for in the beginning, everything God had made was "very good."[6]

They were innocent—how peaceful that would feel—but this condition did not last. Satan came into the garden disguised as *Snake* and before long, Adam and Eve were cast out of Eden into a world where there was jealousy, murder, pain, grief, and old age. There is a place inside each of us that feels deeply offended by this. We seem to know that it should not be this way. God should be near and visible, not far away and mysterious. We yearn for Eden. It makes us restless and unsatisfied with our lives no matter how much or little we have, as if there was a hole in us that we can't seem to fill up with anything less. We even make up our own gods to fill the void. Faced with a life that never quite delivers the real thing, it is no wonder that some of us become hard, angry, and bitter.

Snake comes to each of us in one form or another to take advantage of our hunger and outrage, offering something enticing in exchange for our rebellion. To Eve he offered the prospect of godhood: "you will be like God."[7] For many of us, our agreement with Satan was the defining moment when our life stories really began—our first *kairos*. I had one, and so did you. Our life stories are individually different but in one way or another, we all share a similar experience with Adam and Eve. What approach did *Snake* use when he came to you? I wonder if you thought (as I did) that God must be a monster for making a world like this and then just leaving us here to fend for ourselves. Keep on with this kind of thinking and soon *Snake's* lies make more sense than God's truth does.

I remember a day when an enemy challenged me to a fight on the playground. I was in fifth grade and small for my age. I didn't want to fight him—he was an oversized sixth-grader—but a ring of boys surrounded us, and they wanted to see us fight. I was ringed in and could not run, and then there was my pride. How could I run away in front of all those boys? They started chanting "Fight, fight, fight…" They just kept saying it, and the ring of observers grew thicker and thicker as others ran up to see what was happening.

I remembered what my father taught me about fighting. He said, "You have to disable your enemy with the first blow because you might not get a second chance to hit him." I took my best shot and tried to break the bigger boy's nose with the first punch. His nose bled. I hurt him just enough to make him go berserk but not enough to stop him. After that, the blows fell like rain on my little body. I had the breath knocked out of me and couldn't breathe. With nowhere to run, I curled up on the ground into a ball to protect my face, stomach, and crotch. He kicked me again and again in the ribs, in the hips, and in the head until I passed out. He kept going until the bell rang and his anger was all spent. Then everyone ran for their classrooms. I think I retreated into a place inside myself where I would not feel the pain anymore, someplace a child should never have to go, way, way inside my mind somewhere.

When I woke up, the playground was deserted. The physical pain was bad, but I got over that soon. It was the shame that I couldn't shake. It clung to me for decades. As I limped back toward the school building, I let *Snake* into my heart. I made a vow: *This will never happen to me again.* If I couldn't make myself bigger and stronger than him, I would make myself smarter than him, smarter than *all of them*. I galvanized myself with this. Anger made me feel powerful, like I could do anything if I wanted it enough. I raised my grade point average to 4.0 in seventh and eighth grade. I went to the library during recess and lunch to hide from the bullies. I fantasized that I was a secret agent on an important mission that I couldn't tell anyone. I made sure I knew where the other boys were and always had an escape plan. During the summer I read a book a day, hardly going outside where I might encounter a neighborhood bully. I was on a mission to be smarter and better than anyone who might threaten me in any way. Then I joined a religious cult. It was perfect for me: It had all the answers, an explanation for every mystery, and even secrets. They promised us real power, and so I fell for the same lie that *Snake* used on Eve. Someday, they taught, I would be *a god*. I became a Pharisee, one of those know-it-all, self-righteous people Jesus argued with all the time, one of those people he called a "son of hell."[8]

Why does God put Adam and Eve in a beautiful garden and then allow his enemy to tempt them? Why does he allow them to choose sin? Why does he let us fall, each in our own way? Why are there pain and sickness, crime and abuse, war and death? I don't have all the answers anymore, but I do know that God has a plan for us that we can't see, and that plan is good. He is the one who can take the bad things from life and use them for good.[9] He is preparing each of us to become citizens of a kingdom so wonderful we can't even imagine it; and that preparation requires that we become broken first so he can heal us, that we die to our old life that we hated anyway so he can give us a different kind of life, life with him inside of us, life that matters.

Dear friend in Jesus, I hope and pray that these letters encourage you. Every one of us is wounded, bleeding on the battlefield, about to die. Then we meet Jesus and it changes everything. Even the injustice in our lives can be transformed into something good; making us glad we were born after all, born twice. Maybe not today, but down the road, our stories will start to make sense. Bear in mind that Eden is only chapter one, the setup for a great story yet to unfold. There are more chapters to this story, and each one is set in a different garden. As a believer in Jesus, you can know without seeing that your story has a happy ending, a glorious ending, a surprise-happy-glorious ending as all great stories do.

May the love of the Father who made you, the Son he sent to rescue you, and the Holy Spirit he gives to live within you give you peace and take away your shame.

STUDY QUESTIONS

There is no right answer for any of these. They are here to help you to have a discussion with other believers who have read the letters or for you to deepen your private study of Bible passages we have touched on. I have chosen questions that ask you to look into your own heart and experiences and to put them next to the Word of God. This kind of study is a habit of life that can deepen our relationship and walk with Jesus. Another way to deepen your understanding is to go through the endnotes for each letter and write down your thoughts about them in a journal. A third way to work through the letters is for you to write a reply letter to each one. I would be happy to read those if you do.

Discuss a difficult situation in your life and how God has blessed you through it.

_____

_____

How do the following verses speak to the question of God's motive in allowing us to experience loss?

Genesis 50:20

_____

_____

Romans 5:3–5

_____

_____

James 1:2–4

_____

_____

What was different for Adam and Eve in Eden than for every person who came after them?

_____

_____

What behaviors do people use to fill the emptiness we each feel in our hearts?

_____

_____

Was there a specific time in your life when you let Satan influence you? What disguise did he use?

_____

_____

Below are a few of Satan's lies. What is God's truth about them?

I must meet certain goals in order to feel good about myself (John 6:28–29).

_____

_____

I must be approved by certain others in order to feel good about myself (Romans 14:4).

_____

_____

Those who fail are unworthy of love and deserve to be punished, blamed, or condemned (1 John 4:10).

_____

_____

I am what I am. I cannot change. I am hopeless (2 Corinthians 5:17).

_____

_____

What does the Father say about fighting? (Matthew 5: 39)

_____

_____

Is there a behavior you have used to protect yourself that you would like to change?

_____

_____

LETTER
TWO
The Garden of
King Solomon

My dear friend in Jesus,

I hope this letter finds you well and enjoying day two of your retreat. My home was blessed this week with fifteen new puppies. The mother is a black Labrador, and the papa is a shepherd/heeler mix. Ten puppies are black, and five are chocolate colored. They will be ready to wean and give away in time for Christmas.

Father, I pray that your Holy Spirit will help me write this letter to your beloved. In Jesus's mighty name, amen.

Now we go on to chapter two of the story in which we find the garden of Solomon, King of Israel. The Bible tells us that Solomon was the wisest man ever to live on the earth and that he became the richest king in the world.[10] The books attributed to him are Proverbs (most of it), containing his fatherly advice to his sons; Ecclesiastes, in which he writes of his search for the meaning of life; and the Song of Songs, one of the greatest pieces of literature ever written on romantic love. It is written like a play with different speakers so that it could be performed by actors.

In the Song, there are three characters: a maiden (the beloved), a shepherd (the lover), and the king. Some lines are spoken by a chorus of friends to provide commentary, but this is just the way plays were written in those days. They aren't really in the story.

The beloved, dear friend, is you, the person reading this letter. She is a Shulammite maiden of great beauty but low rank from Lebanon, more than a hundred miles to the north of Jerusalem but within the kingdom of Solomon at that time. She is secretly in love with the king but has no chance to ever meet him, much less for him to take any notice of her. The book begins with her prayer to him:

> Let him kiss me with the kisses of his mouth, for your love is more delightful than wine. Pleasing is the fragrance of your perfumes [kings in those days did wear perfume]; your name is like perfume poured out. No wonder the maidens love you! Take me away with you—let us hurry! Let the king bring me into his chambers.
>
> Song of Songs 1:2–4

Make no mistake about her intentions: the word *chambers* means his bedroom suite; she wants to become his bride. She goes on to describe herself: "Dark am I, yet lovely... do not stare at me because I am dark, because I am darkened by the sun. My mother's sons were angry with me and made me take care of the vineyards; my own vineyard I have neglected."[11] She has been forced by her half-brothers ("my mother's sons" from a different father) to work like a servant. She does their hard work and has no time to make her own living. She is in the same position as Cinderella, dreaming of her prince while she slaves away her days.

The beloved bears some resemblances to us. She lives outside of the country of Israel but in a land that is subject to Solomon. She is a Gentile (not an Israelite) but is as much a subject of the king as any of the twelve tribes. Some people think she represents the church in that we too are Gentiles from a foreign land who have become the subjects of a Jewish king. As such, we also have a father who is not here but in heaven and we live among those who are related to us by blood but have another father: the devil.

The second character, the lover, is a mysterious shepherd who comes and goes but who loves you and desires to be your husband. Every time he comes, he does everything he can to convince you that you should be with him. The secret of this man is that he is Jesus, the Good Shepherd.[12] He "has no place to lay his head"[13]—he sleeps in the field with his flock—but you can tell he really loves you: "I liken you, my darling, to a mare harnessed to one of the chariots of Pharaoh. Your cheeks are beautiful with earrings, your neck with strings of jewels. We will make you earrings of gold studded with silver." He tells you that one day you will have a grand house with beams of cedar and rafters of fir.[14] This is pretty big talk for a shepherd.

Jesus is like the mysterious shepherd. He comes and goes. We have an encounter with him, then it seems like he is gone again. He wants us to follow him and be with him, but we don't know where he is going or how to find him.[15] He makes promises to us that are hard to believe. He talks about the wonderful things he will do for us, but we are still suffering in the heat of someone else's vineyard.

In Song chapter 3, the beloved maiden has fallen in love with her shepherd suitor and pines for him to come back for her. She is so distraught she gets up from her bed before day-light and wanders the dark streets to look for him, heedless of the danger. After inquiring of and passing by the city watch-men, she finds him and clings to him. She accepts his pro-posal of marriage by offering to give herself to him that very night in the bed where her mother conceived her; but for some unknown reason, he declines to take her away just yet.

In the next scene, something very unusual happens in her city. They see the dust rising from a fast-approaching military party on the horizon and say, "Who is this coming up from the desert like a column of smoke?"[16] This imagery evokes the Exodus, during which the Lord appeared to Israel as a pillar of smoke that went before them. Long after Solomon died, Isaiah asks a similar question by saying, "Who is this coming from Edom, from Bozrah with his garments stained crimson?"[17] On that day, the Old Testament says they will realize that the one who was crucified is also the Messiah, their promised king.[18]

"Look! It is Solomon's carriage, escorted by sixty warriors, the noblest of Israel, all of them wearing the sword, all expe-rienced in battle, each with his sword by his side, prepared for the terrors of the night."[19] Here comes the king himself in his royal carriage with an honor guard of knights. What could he possibly be doing so far from Jerusalem? The door of the carriage opens, and he is wearing his royal crown. Then some-thing wonderful happens. The king steps down and looks directly at you, dear beloved, and says, "How beautiful you are, my darling! Oh, how beautiful!" He then describes your beauty in poetic detail in front of everyone. It's clear from his lan-guage that he too is looking forward to your wedding night. He says again, "How beautiful you are my darling, there is no flaw in you. Come with me from Lebanon... you have stolen my heart, my sister, my bride; you have stolen my heart with one glance of your eyes!"[20]

To your surprise, here is the king, and he is the same man who came to you before as the simple shepherd. He was in disguise all along. He wanted to know if you would love him as a poor shepherd first before it was safe for him to reveal that he is really the king you dreamed of and prayed to. He wanted to be sure you loved him for himself, not for his riches and glory. You did; and he came back to take you away to his palace, where it turns out he has a private garden.

Do you find it strange that he calls you "my sister, my bride?" Keep in mind that when we give our hearts to Jesus, we become sons and daughters of God.[21] We now have the same Father that Jesus has. We are truly his sister and his bride at the same time. We can leave behind the evil brothers who held us in bondage; we have been adopted into the king's own family. All he has is also ours to share with him. Did you catch the part about "there is no flaw in you"? He has paid for your sins. Because he did, there is no condemnation for you at all.[22] No matter what your life was like before you knew him, you are flawless in his eyes. All he wants from you is your undivided heart.

I would expect that after riding to Jerusalem with the king, *you* would enter into *his* garden, but the passage says just the opposite. In Song 4:12, he says, "You are a garden locked up, my sister, my bride; you are a spring enclosed, a sealed fountain."

How can you be his garden? After you receive him, he lives in you.[23] *You* are *his* place of peace and rest; the place of privacy inside your heart is where his love can grow. He would rather be in your heart than anywhere else. A garden must have a wall to keep it private and safe. He has locked you and kept the key for himself. You have a spring of living water inside you, just as any garden must have fresh water for the plants that grow there. You are his sealed fountain.[24]

In John 4:4–42, Jesus is speaking to a Samaritan woman whose life has been destroyed by compromise, a woman who lives with shame every day. She comes to the well to draw water during the hottest part of the day, possibly so she could avoid being there when the other women came. Jesus says to her, "Will you give me a drink?" She tries to blow him off by saying, "Aren't you a Jew?" Jesus presses her, "If you knew who it is that asks you for a drink, you would have asked him and he would have given you living water." When we follow Jesus, he becomes like a fountain of living water inside us. He refreshes us when we get dry and thirsty.

THE FRUITS IN SOLOMON'S GARDEN

Solomon names nine fruits in his garden: pomegranates, henna, nard, saffron, calamus, cinnamon, incense, myrrh, and aloes (Song 4:13–14). This is interesting because Paul lists exactly nine fruits of the Holy Spirit: love, joy, peace, patience, kindness, goodness, faithfulness, gentleness, and self-control (Galatians 5:22–23). If the Holy Spirit is in us, we will also have some of his fruit. The longer he is in us the more mature the plants become that bear them and the more of them we will have. Let's look at the fruit of the spirit list from Galatians and set it side by side with the fruits in Solomon's garden. You can decide for yourself whether these two passages are talking about the same things.

FRUIT ONE: LOVE

Pomegranate is a red fruit that makes a tart red juice that, when mixed with wine, makes a marvelous drink the color of blood.

Jesus demonstrated his love for us by pouring out his blood.[25] The seeds of this fruit even look like large drops of blood. The hem of the high priest's robe was decorated with pomegranates and golden bells.[26] Jesus is our high priest;[27] he is dressed with pomegranates as symbols of his love. The pillars of the temple were also decorated with two hundred pomegranates around the tops.[28] Paul says we are the temple;[29] Jesus adorns us also with the symbols of his love. *Pom* means "apple." We are the apple of our Lord's eye.[30] Red still symbolizes love today: red hearts, red roses, red candy, red lipstick.

FRUIT TWO: JOY

Henna is a fragrant white flower that grows in clusters. White represents purity, as in the white robes of the redeemed.[31] This is the purity of Christ that covers us and produces joy in us even in difficulty and hardship. No one can take away a believer's joy because no one can take us away from Jesus.[32] Henna is made into camphor, a medicine used to waken a person who has fainted. When our hearts faint, Jesus is our camphor. The joy of knowing we are secure in him revives us.

FRUIT THREE: PEACE

Nard (NIV) or *spikenard* (KJV) is the perfume with which Jesus was anointed at a dinner in Simon the leper's house at Bethany.[33] Jesus said the woman who poured it on him anointed him for his burial. It is very costly to make nard. The peace Jesus has given us with God was also very costly! A medicine of it called valerian is still used today as a tranquilizer to calm people and help them sleep. Jesus is our nard who allows us to rest in peace with God.

The passage lists nard twice for emphasis. Jesus also says it twice when he says, "Peace I leave with you; my peace I give you."[34]

FRUIT FOUR: PATIENCE

Saffron means "yellow." It is a flower from the crocus family. The stamens are used for making yellow dye, perfumes, and flavoring for food. Yellow is the color we associate with waiting. In August 1983, when Cory Aquino's husband, Benigno "Ninoy" Aquino, was returning home from the United States to the Philippines, yellow ribbons were tied by his allies in Manila as a sign that they still believed in him as their elected leader to oppose the dictator Ferdinand Marcos. This sign was taken from the song "Tie a Yellow Ribbon Round the Old Oak Tree" in which a man getting out of prison asked his beloved to mark the old tree with a yellow ribbon if she was still waiting faithfully for him to return. Mature believers learn to wait on God. It leads to the next fruit.

FRUIT FIVE: KINDNESS

Calamus is also called sweet flag or sweet cane, a sweet scent used in expensive perfumes and one of the ingredients of the holy anointing oil.[35] Kindness must also be an ingredient in the character of the believer. The Lord expected sacrifices to have a pleasing (NIV) or sweet (KJV) odor.[36] Paul said we are to present our bodies as a living sacrifice.[37] God wants to see kindness in the sacrifices we make for him. Some teachers point to the anointing oil as symbolic of the anointing of the Holy Spirit. When a person shows kindness while others are attacking them, it is a clear sign that the person is being controlled by the Spirit of God.

FRUIT SIX: GOODNESS

Cinnamon is another ingredient of the holy anointing oil. It comes from the inner bark of the cinnamon tree. It has a sharp flavor and a clean aroma. It isn't sweet but mixes with sugar agreeably. Goodness is having the backbone to do the right thing when it isn't easy or popular, but goodness by itself has the potential to make enemies of the very people we hope to bring to Jesus. When goodness and kindness are mingled, it inspires people and pleases God. Paul elsewhere points out that goodness without love is worthless.[38]

FRUIT SEVEN: FAITHFULNESS

Incense (NIV) or *frankincense* (KJV) is a dry, aromatic gum from a tree that grows in Arabia that gives off its odor freely (frankly) when burned, hence its name. It burns for a long time with a steady flame. It was unlawful in Israel to burn incense except for priests,[39] and then only in the holy place of the temple twice daily. One day a year, on *Yom Kippur,* the high priest burned incense and went into the holy of holies, into the presence of the Lord and the Ark of the Covenant to sprinkle the blood of the sin offering onto the mercy seat. The purpose of the incense was to fill the apartment with smoke to keep the high priest from looking with too much curiosity on the ark and so die.[40] While the incense was being offered, the worshippers outside offered their prayers, which ascended to the Lord with the sweet odor of the incense until the high priest returned and gave the blessing: "Your sins are forgiven, go in peace." Jesus is our frankincense because he presents our prayers to God and bestows the blessing of forgiveness. As the smoke of the incense protected the high priest from the holiness of God, faith in Jesus conveys us safely into the presence of God, where we may address him "frankly" in prayer. Paul elsewhere compares faith to a shield.[41] The Magi brought three gifts for the baby Jesus: gold for his kingship, incense for his high priesthood, and myrrh for his death as the Lamb of God.[42]

FRUIT EIGHT: GENTLENESS OR MEEKNESS

Myrrh was a principal ingredient for making the holy anointing oil.[43] *Gentleness* (NIV) or *meekness* (KJV) is translated from *prautes,* which has no true English equivalent. According to Aristotle, this word is the middle ground between two extremes, getting angry without reason, and not getting angry at all; it is *anger under control.* In the worldly sense, a gentleman is a man who controls his passions. In the spiritual sense, gentleness is an inward grace by which we accept God's dealings with us as good and do not dispute or resist.[44] To be gentle or meek means to deny selfish desires and do what is required of you.[45] Esther was bathed in oil of myrrh for six months before she could be allowed into the presence of the king.[46] She meekly went before the king to her probable death to save the lives of all Jews, foreshadowing Christ.[47] Myrrh was used for embalming as one of the only perfumes strong enough to overcome the stench of death.[48] It must be crushed to extract its potent odor. Jesus is our myrrh because he was "crushed for our iniquities"[49] and overcame death itself by meekly going to the cross. Myrrh was used as a narcotic to numb the pain of crucifixion and hasten death, but Jesus refused it.[50] He robs death of its sting better than a narcotic.[51]

FRUIT NINE: SELF-CONTROL

Aloe comes from either the juice or the hardened resin of an East Indian tree that yields a rich perfume, also called aloe wood, paradise wood, or eagle wood, of such rarity to be worth its weight in gold. It was used by Egyptians as a preservative for embalming. Nicodemus bought about a hundred pounds of aloe and myrrh for the burial of Jesus, a kingly gift.[52] Solomon said self-control is easily worth more than gold and is just as rare.[53] Paul said self-control acts as a preservative to keep believers from continually running back to their old sins.[54] Jesus is our aloe, who preserves us through trials and temptations.

I think this listing of fruits in the Song of Songs points to the fruit of the Spirit because of the next verse. The beloved says, "Awake, north wind, and come, south wind! Blow on my garden, that its fragrance may spread abroad. Let my lover come into his garden and taste its choice fruits" (Song 4:16). If I were out in my garden, I would not normally pray for wind, so why is that here?

In the Bible, wind or breath is also used to represent the Holy Spirit. Jesus breathed on his apostles, and they received the Holy Spirit.[55] On the day of Pentecost, a mighty rushing wind came from heaven and filled the whole house where the followers of Jesus were praying.[56] The Spirit fell on them all, and they spoke in languages that they had never spoken before. The Jews ran together to see what the noise was and heard them praising God in every different language in the Roman world. When we ask Jesus to "blow on my garden," we are asking him to fill us with the Holy Spirit. This causes the fragrance of the fruit of the Spirit to attract the attention of people around us. They wonder where all that kindness and patience comes from when we should be bitter and angry like they are. The Spirit of God gives us the ability to speak in a language that others can understand so they can hear what he has done for us. By this means, the work of God in our hearts is spread abroad.

Now, dear friend in Jesus, my letter is very long. I will simply pray that there is something in it to feed your spirit. Tomorrow, we will visit a very different kind of garden.

STUDY QUESTIONS

Does God promise you anything in the Bible that you find hard to believe?

_____

_____

Is there a particular promise that you take comfort from?

_____

_____

What does the love story in the Song tell us about God's love for us?

_____

_____

If we are the Lord's private garden, how do you suppose he prepares us before he plants the different fruit-bearing plants of his Spirit?

_____

_____

Is there one fruit of the Spirit that stands out for you? Why?

_____

_____

Are any of the fruits that Paul talked about missing in your life?

_____

_____

Is there anything you can do to produce this fruit, or is it entirely a work of God?

_____

_____

Ask the Holy Spirit to fill you either in your own words or with this prayer:

Father, I believe in your son, Jesus, and receive him as my Lord and Savior. I accept his death on the cross as the complete payment for my sins. (If you do not believe you are forgiven for something you have done, confess it now.) Thank you for forgiving me and for giving me new life. Fill me now with your Holy Spirit so that I can grow in your love and so I can show that kind of love to everyone I meet. Holy Spirit, come.

PHOTO BY GREG BRAVE – WWW.PHOTOPATHWAY.COM

LETTER THREE

The Garden of Gethsemane

My dear friend in Jesus,

This third letter is to encourage you in the dark night of the soul. I ask the Father to send his Spirit into the words I write and into your heart as you read them, in the mighty name of his son, Jesus.

Chapter three in this story of God's love takes us into another garden called Gethsemane (Aramaic: *Gat-Shemanim*), which means "oil press" or "crushing place." It was night, and Jesus had already prepared his disciples for his death as much as he could. By this time the next day, his disfigured and lifeless body would be laying in the tomb of Joseph, the rich man who went to Pilate to ask for it.[57] The Bible tells us that Jesus went to this garden often to pray. It was across from the East wall of Jerusalem on a low hill facing the temple and contained an orchard of olive trees that stand there to this very day. There was not much safety there with the low wall and no locking gate. He came there to prepare himself to die for every sin ever committed, both past and future.

Judas had gone out into the night earlier to make contact with those who wanted Jesus dead. He had heard Jesus predict his death several times and, apparently, could not stand it anymore. They had gone through all the towns and villages in Judah and Galilee to announce the kingdom of God, and now their king-in-waiting was taking a turn for the worst. Weren't any of the other apostles paying attention? *Snake* had a better idea; and when it was over, Judas would be the appropriately humble hero, the savior of all they were working toward. If Jesus were to be taken by his enemies, he would be forced to use his God powers to take control of the city, and that would bring in the kingdom right away. Judas could not understand or agree with what God was doing, so he took matters into his own hands. Maybe he decided God needed his help to do the right thing.

The other eleven apostles were tired. They had a long day, an emotional supper with their master, full stomachs, and a fair amount of wine on board. Eight of them bedded down near the entrance to the garden, and three went further into the garden with Jesus when he asked them to stay awake and watch. For the first time in his life, Jesus asked his father to give him a way out of doing what he had been born to do; but unlike Judas, he controlled his selfish feelings. He was meek when he had every reason to rebel. As he moved deeper into his ordeal, his friends nodded off.[58] Luke says an angel came to strengthen him. "And being in anguish, he prayed more earnestly, and his sweat was like drops of blood falling to the ground."[59] No one can say if his sweat looked like blood in the dark or if it really was blood; but what is clear is that he was undergoing tremendous strain, as if *he* was being crushed in the press. After this, he went back into prayer the third time and made his contract with his father.

I will let you into a secret about real men that many women do not appreciate enough. Men express their deepest feelings by their actions more than by showing emotions or talking about them. A man's highest expression of love is to be ready at any moment to sacrifice himself to protect a loved one. Jesus said there is no greater love in the world than the love of a man who would willingly die to save you.[60] Jesus was not a weak man—not afraid to die on a cross to save us—but what he was facing was more than that. As God, he knew this would be different. He was to bear the sin of the entire world when he went to the cross and receive the full punishment from God for all of it.[61] He would take the place of Genghis Kahn, Adolph Hitler, Pol Pot, every dictator, every criminal, everyone, all of us and receive the full punishment. Only a God could do such a thing. The big question is, *why would he?*

There's more. Jesus was without sin. He hated sin. He abhorred it, yet now was being covered with it. You see guys on reality TV covered with snakes or worms or bugs. You see people covered in raw sewage on some of these shows, but this was far worse. Paul wrote, "God made him who had no sin to be sin for us."[62] Jesus *became* sin for us. No wonder he was sweating! Why would he do this? I think the answer was back there in Solomon's garden. He wanted to be with us like a man in love wants his bride; no sacrifice would be too great. I hear the music: *"No mountain is high enough, no ocean is wide enough"* ... *"I would walk five hundred miles"* ... you know the love songs; and for Jesus, they are true. For this, he came down from heaven, humbled himself, and took our place on judgment day.[63]

Imagine you are in a courtroom and the jury has found you guilty on all counts. The judge gives you the maximum sentence, no mercy. Then imagine that he gets up, removes his robe, comes down where you are, and tells the guards to take him away in your place so you can go free. We say that the God of the Old Testament was harsh and intolerant but fail to remember that it was his own flesh he planned to zap with his holiness, not the people. When they sacrificed a lamb, they were covered.

In Eden, Adam and Eve tried to force the hand of God by eating the fruit of the tree of knowledge. Perhaps, like Judas, they thought they knew what needed to happen; they were going to help God get it right. Then they looked down and, for the first time, realized they were naked. They were filled with shame and tried to cover their nakedness by sewing together fig leaves. When God came to the garden in the cool of the day, they hid from him. People make a mistake when they follow a religion to find God. He lives in heaven, where no person can ever find him; he had to come down and *find us*. He called out, "Adam, where are you?"[64] He came down to us in our sin to save us. In Eden, the Lord made coats of skins for Adam and Eve to clothe them.[65] That probably meant he had to kill live animals to get the skins. I don't think man introduced death into the world; it was God. He did this to illustrate that the penalty for sin is death—blood will be spilt—and then he came down and gave every drop of his own blood. *What kind of love does this?*

I was eleven years old. I was taking out the garbage after school to the cans by the side of our house. It was a fenced enclosure—a tiny paradise, if you will—one of the few really private places around our house. I had started out the year feeling this hole in myself. I wanted to find God. I went to different churches in my neighborhood and with my Catholic best friend to Mass and to Catechism. I drove the nun crazy with all my questions. She said, "Many of these things are a mystery." I said, "That's okay. When you see God, just ask him for me. Then you can tell me next week." I meant every word, but she thought I was mocking her. In my young mind, I thought the hood and robe and cross she wore meant that she was holy and could just talk with God anytime she wanted. I didn't know anything. I felt so shamed and disillusioned by her angry reaction that I never went back.

So here I was by the garbage cans at my house, and I felt this prayer well up from my innermost heart: *God, I can't find you! Please find me!* That was it. I did not come forward for an altar call. I believe God heard me cry out and took me in like an orphan. I think that was the day I was saved, or at least it was the start of it—my second *kairos*.[66] Since that day, I have nearly always had this childlike trust that God hears me when I pray. I know he is listening because he did answer my prayer that day and countless other prayers since then. It doesn't happen often; but once in a while, he says something and *I hear Him.*

In the garden of Gethsemane, at around midnight, Judas came along with "a detachment of soldiers and officials from the chief priests and Pharisees." Now, Jesus was as cool as a cucumber. He said, "Who do you want?" They said, "Jesus of Nazareth." He answered, "I am he."[67] I think his actual words were, "I AM," which, for Jews, was the name of God.[68] What happened next is never shown in the movies about Jesus; but John writes, "When Jesus said, 'I am he,' they drew back and fell to the ground. Again, he asked them 'Who is it you want?' And they said [from the ground], 'Jesus of Nazareth'" (John 18:6).

Here is a small army of soldiers and officials; and at the sound of Jesus saying, "I AM," they all fall down and can't get up. Peter grabs his sword and attacks, cutting off the ear of the high priest's servant, Malchus, but he was no soldier. It was a badly aimed blow. Jesus tells him, "Put your sword back in its place … Do you think I cannot call on my father, and he will at once put at my disposal more than twelve legions of angels?"[69] Then he reaches down and restores the missing ear of the guy arresting him. Do we see a poor mistreated figure or do we see the Son of the living God standing here, with his enemies lying prostrate? He tells them, "If you are looking for me, then let these men go." The apostles were able to run away while the soldiers were getting back up. Mark said there was a young man there who almost lingered too long. It was probably himself: "A young man, wearing nothing but a tunic was following Jesus. When they seized him, he fled naked, leaving his garment behind."[70]

Two gardens, two naked men running away from God; first Adam, now Mark. These men were ashamed of themselves for running away, but God was there in both gardens to cover them. He sacrificed innocent animals to make coats of skins for Adam and Eve. He went to the cross to cover Mark. God covers our nakedness. He covers our shame by shedding his own blood.

When Jesus died, his last words were, "It is finished!"[71] In his language, that also means "Paid in full!" In today's vernacular it could mean, "I've covered it." He's got us covered. We don't have to live in shame anymore; we can have peace and joy. Even in prison, you can have this peace and joy that no one can ever take away.

Dear friend in Jesus, God bless you this night with the absolute assurance that he has you covered.

STUDY QUESTIONS

Have you ever felt that God needed your help or that you had to make things happen a certain way?   Yes   No

If your answer is yes, what did you do and how did it work out for you?

_____

_____

What do you think caused Jesus so much sorrow while he prayed in Gethsemane? Was it that he knew he would die in agony, or was it something even worse?

_____

_____

Think of a love song that would be an exaggeration for a man to say, but is true for Jesus.

_____

_____

Describe a situation where you were shown mercy.

_____

_____

Where did God come to find you? Did you feel naked before him?

_____

_____

Now that he has covered you, do you feel that you can talk with God any time?

_____

_____

ART BY DUNCAN LONG – WWW.DUNCANLONG.COM

LETTER FOUR

The Garden of
New Jerusalem

My dear friend in Jesus,

I am writing this letter for day four of your retreat. I hope it has been a fruitful time for you and that you have experienced the love of the volunteers as well as the love of God. It isn't a natural thing to love complete strangers, people you have not even met. Jesus said that people would recognize his disciples because of the love they had for each other.[72] I hope you have felt it and know how real it is.

I have to confess that I'm a lot more comfortable behind a computer or stack of books than I am with people unless I know them very well. I play the bass guitar in church—that is safe enough—and I like to pray for people; it's easier than talking with them. I hope I have not offended or bored you in these letters. The truth is I care about you and what you are going through. I also really, really love Jesus. Life without him would not be worth living. I like to read the Bible and look for patterns in it, like this series on God's gardens. I hope you find it encouraging (en-*courage*-ing). Have courage because you know who you are in Jesus. I have to find my courage in him too.

The next garden is in the final act of this play, the grand finale. We have a surprisingly big role to play in it. Parts of it are told in the book of Revelation, and parts are hinted at in other books of the Bible. You can't just turn to one particular chapter. This is the garden of the heavenly city, the New Jerusalem. All the other gardens are just a cheap imitation of this one. This is Paradise, the place we usually just call heaven.

In Revelation chapter one, John meets Jesus resurrected. Even after all the time they spent together, John is overcome by the glory of his Lord. Jesus tells John he wants him to take down a letter to the seven churches. By this time, John was old. He had taken Mary, the mother of Jesus, with him and moved up to western Turkey. In those days, it was called the Roman Province of Asia or Asia Minor. John was the elder over seven churches that were all on the same mail route for the Roman letter carriers. If you followed that route, you would come to each of the towns where a church was in the same order Jesus dictated his letters.

Revelation chapters 2 and 3 contain the letters Jesus sent to the seven churches. They are remarkable because when we look back at the history of the church, they appear to have anticipated it prophetically. When you read these letters, it can be interesting to ask, "Which of the seven churches do I belong to?" When I read them, I feel like I was part of the synagogue of Satan in the letter to Philadelphia. Jesus said, "I will make those who are of the synagogue of Satan, who claim to be Jews though they are not, but are liars—I will make them come and fall down at your feet and acknowledge that I have loved you."[73]

After my disillusionment with the churches in my neighborhood, I joined and belonged to a cult for twenty-five years that believed we were spiritual Israel and had taken the place of the Jews as God's chosen people. Each member who was worthy was declared by a special priesthood holder to belong to one of the twelve tribes of Israel. My tribe was Ephraim. I remember feeling proud about that, as if it was somehow better than any other tribe. There was this whole belief about how the lost tribes of Israel were scattered throughout the world and we had some of their blood in us, but the truth is that I am 100 percent white Anglo-Saxon Gentile and my belief that I had become an Israelite (or Jew) of the tribe of Ephraim was a lie. This cult believes it is the only denomination that God accepts, but Jesus says here that one day he will make them kneel and admit he loves the rest of his church. Fourteen years ago, I left them and came and knelt in another church to fulfill this prophesy. I did come forward to the altar at that time to ask for forgiveness and salvation in Jesus Christ alone. I wanted to be sure.

THE SEVEN CHURCHES

I should explain what I mean when I say the letters to the seven churches look like they anticipated Christian history. Some Jewish rabbis teach that God's Word is to be understood on three levels: the immediate or historical meaning, the prophetic or messianic meaning, and the personal application or spiritual meaning. These letters have all three. Jesus sent them to seven real churches with real problems and triumphs, but I want to look at them as a summary of Christian history given in advance by our Savior to give us his perspective on how we are doing. Let me warn you, if we are honest, each of us should find something in here to make us squirm.

CHURCH ONE: EPHESUS (REVELATION 2:1–7)

Ephesus means "my darling." It was John's home church after he left Jerusalem, and it was where Mary, the mother of Jesus, lived at the end of her life. During part of the first century AD, the church was so full of love that they sold whatever land or extra property they had to care for each other.[74] It was largely a house church and grew quickly. They did not have a complete New Testament yet but relied on the teaching of the apostles.[75] Over time, their love grew cooler, but at least they rejected the Nicolaitians. That word means *Nica'o* ("to rule over") plus *laity* ("the common members"). They rejected those who promoted having a priestly class to rule over them. Jesus promises them the right to eat of the tree of life in Paradise. This promise is significant because that was the tree in Eden that God kept Adam and Eve away from with guardian angels and a floating flaming sword after they sinned.[76]

CHURCH TWO: SMYRNA (REVELATION 2:8–11)

Smyrna means "city of myrrh." Myrrh is associated with death and burial, as we saw in the fruits of Solomon's garden. This letter provides a hint that these letters might be prophesy when Jesus mentions ten days of suffering persecution and imprisonment for this church. During the second and third centuries AD, there were ten Roman emperors who tried to kill off the church: Nero, Domitian, Trajan, Marcus Aurelius, Septimus, Maximus, Decius, Valerian, Aurelian, and Diocletian. Smyrna might also represent Christians who are under persecution in subsequent centuries, including the present one. Jesus promises them the crown of life. In the Olympic Games, it was customary to crown the victor with a wreath made of laurel branches, and the image given here is similar. Today, we would say the Smyrna believers were awarded the gold medal for their faithfulness under extreme pressure.

CHURCH THREE: PERGAMUM
(REVELATION 2:12–17)

Pergamum is a compound of two words, *Per* ("mixed") plus *gamy* ("marriage"). In Jewish law, mixing the holy with the profane (or clean with unclean) was called perversion. Clean things are *kosher* ("blessed") if they are not allowed to touch unclean things. Mixed marriages between Israelites and foreigners were strictly forbidden as not *kosher* or not blessed of God. This name suggests the mixed or unlawful marriage between the holy church and the unholy Roman Empire under Constantine and his successors in the third to sixth centuries AD. Some citizens were forced to accept Christianity by Constantius II, a thing of which the Lord did not approve. Antipas, who is mentioned in this letter, was the bishop of Pergamum and was executed for the stand he took against pagan worship. The city boasted a huge statue of Zeus on a throne much like the Lincoln Monument in Washington, DC, which Jesus calls Satan's throne. Jesus recalls when the traitor prophet Balaam took a bribe from Moab's King Balak to teach him how to remove God's blessing from Israel so his army could defeat them by enticing the young men of Israel to engage in pagan worship (free food and sex) and then take home the Moabite girls as wives.[77] God's blessing was similarly removed from the church when it became married to the Roman Empire that worshipped Zeus. Jesus does not like the emergence of a priestly clergy (the Nicolaitians) to rule over the church. Today, the successor of this marriage is the Eastern Orthodox branch of the church. Jesus promises them the hidden manna (the free food of Jesus, the bread of life[78]) instead of the unholy food of pagan worship, together with a new name. When a woman marries, she takes a new name, so this might refer to this church's future as part of the bride of Christ.

CHURCH FOUR: THYATIRA
(REVELATION 2:18–28)

Thyatira was the mother goddess of the Hittites, also known in various languages as Ashtoreth, Asherah, or Estar. She holds a place in the pagan pantheon equivalent to Rhea (wife of Cronus and mother of Zeus), Hera (wife of Zeus and mother of Ares/Mars), Isis (wife of Osiris and mother of Horus), and other similar goddesses as the queen of heaven. Her origin is thought to have been from Semiramus, the wife of Nimrod who built the tower of Babel in defiance of God.[79] Nimrod was called the "mighty hunter," either for driving away the large wild animals in Shinar, or for being a hunter of men to follow him. With his popularity as a leader, he built the first world empire in Babylon (Iraq) and instituted worship of the gods and goddesses of the stars. When he died, Semiramus had no right to rule in his place; so she conspired with the priests to create a reincarnation myth to secure the first dynasty for her son Tammuz, who was later called Lord or *Baal.* The mother-son cult of Ashtoreth and Baal, with their sexual worship practices, were popular during much of the Old Testament in opposition to the worship of Yahweh and continued on into Greek and Roman paganism in New Testament times. When Christianity was adopted by pagan Rome, many had difficulty seeing the difference. They adored Mary as the queen of heaven who was depicted in art wearing a crown. The Roman Catholic branch of the church has long tolerated a variety of heresies Jesus compares in his letter to Israel tolerating the foreign queen Jezebel, who married Israel's King Ahab.[80] She dominated Ahab and turned Israel to the worship of Ashtoreth and Baal. One mark of this church is sexual immorality, and Jesus says he will judge her for it. It is amazing how this has even been the case in the problems the Roman Catholic Church has been having with immoral priests. The deep secrets Jesus tells the church to stay away from could include the controversial Fatima Secrets finally published in full in June of 2000, a prophesy that appears to predict the fall of the church in the end times. To the faithful of this church, he promises authority to rule and to see his face, the *morning* star, instead of the gods and goddesses of the nighttime stars.

CHURCH FIVE: SARDIS (REVELATION 3:1–6)

Sardis is a gemstone the color of blood that was carried or worn by Roman soldiers as a talisman for fierceness in battle. It speaks of war and bloodshed. Christians began declaring war on other Christians at the time of the Protestant Reformation. There had been bloodshed before that, but not on this scale. Much blood was spilt in Germany, France, the Netherlands, and Eastern Europe in the 1500s and early 1600s. The modern successors to the Great Reformation are the denominations of Protestantism, a church that remains fractured to this very day. Jesus tells them they have a reputation for being alive, but they are actually dead; they characteristically resist any "unsanctioned" activity of the Holy Spirit. Jesus warns this church that they will be caught unprepared when he comes "like a thief," causing me to wonder if some of them will be saved when they die but left behind when the rapture happens. Jesus promises the faithful of this church white clothing to wear in heaven. This is interesting because the saints who endure the Great Tribulation on earth will also be "given a white robe."[81]

CHURCH SIX: PHILADELPHIA
(REVELATION 3:7–13)

Philadelphia means "city of brotherly love." Jesus says he has placed an open door in front of it that no one can shut. I don't know if this is a reference to salvation, the rapture, or both. I say this because of the door John sees standing open in heaven in Revelation 4:1, which we will come to shortly. The open-door church is one in which a call to salvation is frequently made, and anyone can come forward to belong at any time. Many churches today fit this description, so it might also characterize the church in the time we are living in now. Jesus says that this church has *little strength*. That is the opposite of having *much strength*, as can be seen by how little impact Christianity has made on modern society, especially in the last two centuries. In this part of church history, Jesus identifies a faction that Satan has hold over that claim they are Jews but really aren't. As I mentioned earlier, this could be a reference to replacement theology, which says the church has replaced Israel. Many of the groups that hold this view remain separate by choice from the rest of the body of Christian faith. Jesus says he will one day make them see and admit they are wrong about thinking they are better than other Christians, but there is no warning that they will not be forgiven and saved. Jesus tells this church he is coming soon and promises to "keep [take away, remove] them from the hour of trial that will come upon the whole world," another hint that the rapture might come in our time. He will write on this church the name of God, the name of the New Jerusalem, and "my new name." To be identified with his name and his Father's name when he comes to rule will be as great an honor as anyone could wish for.

CHURCH SEVEN: LAODICEA
(REVELATION 3:14–22)

Laodicea means "ruled by the people." It was a wealthy city known for making a costly medicine for diseases of the eyes. They had two sources of water, one a mineral hot spring and the other an ice-fed stream. The wealthy people lived where the water was either hot or cold, but the poor lived downstream, where it mixed together and was neither good for bathing nor drinking. The mineral salts in the lukewarm water would make it taste bitter indeed. This is a church that has plenty of money, and as the name implies, does its own thing. I imagine a church where the people up on the stage preach loudly, drive expensive cars, are wearing expensive clothing and jewelry, and have big hair. It may also include the emerging church with its rock concert style of worship, watered-down message, and arena-sized meeting places. Jesus compares them to their city, where it is good to be on the hot spring or the ice-fed spring, but if you live downstream, you must be one of the poor. They—or is it we?—are lukewarm in faith, or poor in the things that Jesus cares about. He says the way they taste makes him want to puke. He tells them/us to seek a different kind of gold that comes from God's discipline in our life, white clothes of purity to cover our nakedness (like Adam and Mark), and the healing balm that only Jesus has to open our eyes to what really matters. I am chilled by the next verse: Jesus says he is standing at the door, knocking.[82] What door? The door of the church; and he is *outside*, waiting to be invited in. He promises to come into every heart that opens to him and to share the communion meal of bread and wine with us. He will give the faithful of this church a place to sit with him on *his* throne, not our own thrones. The church resembling this one today can be none other than our own sorry selves in the United States and other wealthy countries. We have little of the richness of spirit seen in so-called poor countries.

SNATCHING AWAY THE CHURCH

Right after the letters to the seven churches, the church apparently leaves the earth. In Revelation 4:1, John hears a voice like a trumpet saying, "Come up here!" And in the blink of an eye, he is standing before the throne of God in heaven. After that, the *church* is never mentioned again as being on earth, even though other believers are. You get a better picture of this event from Paul's first letter to the Thessalonians. He says that the Lord will come down from heaven with a loud voice and the sound of a trumpet and will first raise the dead who died in Christ. "After that, we who are still alive and are left will be caught up together with them in the clouds to meet the Lord in the air. And so we will be with the Lord forever."[83] The word Paul uses for "caught up" is *harpatzo* in Greek or *rapturo* in Latin, which is why we call it the rapture of the church. *Rapturo* means to seize by force, to snatch away. It is the way you would snatch a child from the street to keep him from being hit by a car.

When Peter, Andrew, James, and John asked Jesus to tell them about the signs of his return, he told them it will be just like it was in the days of Lot.[84] We find this story in Genesis 13, 18, and 19. Lot's father was Abraham's brother, Haran. After Haran and their father Terah died, Abraham took Lot with him and moved to Canaan.[85] They both grew wealthy in flocks and servants until they had so much livestock there was not enough feed and water for them all. They decided to split up to make more room. Abraham went up to the Judean hills, and Lot went down to the plain of the Jordan River. At that time it was "well-watered, like the garden of the Lord."[86] Who could blame him if the place was like Eden? He pitched his tent near the city of Sodom. Sodom was so wicked that the Lord decided to destroy it. The only thing holding him back was that Lot was there. The Lord told Abraham what he was planning to do. Like Christ, who interceded with God to save us, Abraham bargained with the Lord for the city of Sodom to save his nephew, Lot. In the end, the Lord sent angels to get Lot out of Sodom so he could destroy it.

PHOTO BY KEVIN FISHER – WWW.ARKDISCOVERY.COM

When God destroyed Sodom and the cities of the plain, he rained down burning sulfur stones the size of golf balls that are still there, imbedded in the walls. That lovely "well-watered" plain became the Dead Sea. Nothing has been able to grow or live there ever since. The probable remains of Sodom and her four sister cities have been located along the shoreline and on the sea floor. Lot did not really want to leave; the angels practically had to drag him out. They snatched him away in the nick of time; they *raptured* him. Lot's wife disobeyed the angel's warning not to look back. When she did, she turned into a pillar of salt.[87] The fact that Lot escaped but his wife did not suggests the possibility that not everyone sitting in the church pews will be taken to heaven in the rapture. As man and wife they were one body (as is the Church), but only Lot and his daughters were rescued alive. Some of the parables of Jesus come to mind: the parable of the weeds in the field,[88] the net that caught good and bad fish,[89] or the parable of the ten virgins,[90] to name a few. If Lot is a type of the Church, then Lot's wife may be a type of those who are left behind at the rapture.

I'm not saying the rapture will allow the church to escape trouble either. More Christians have lost their lives due to religious persecution in the last century than in the nineteen centuries that preceded it, and the worst might be yet to come. But a day will come when God is going to clean house, and whatever he finds that is not the way he wants it will have to go. The promise of the rapture is that, having already been cleansed by the blood of his son and taken over by his Spirit, we will not need to pass through the general cleanup and takeover of earth that will accompany his return.

As Solomon came to take his bride to Jerusalem, Jesus comes to take us to New Jerusalem, the place we usually call heaven without even thinking. I don't know why we have gotten away from calling it Paradise. Jesus told the robber on the cross next to his, "Today you shall be with me in Paradise."[91] The believing criminal never had a chance to get baptized, go to a church, or pay tithing. He never did anything good; he only admitted his guilt and asked Jesus, in his guise as the lowly shepherd, to remember him when he returns as the king. He still had to endure the sentence for his crimes while in this body, but putting his faith in Jesus *plus nothing* was enough to save his soul from hell—enough for any of us. This gives me hope that believers left behind at the rapture for whatever reason will still be saved when they die.

PARADISE

What is Paradise like? Paul mentions seeing it. He had been stoned and probably died, or at least he seemed dead.[92] The believers prayed over him, and God raised him, but he was forbidden to write what he saw and heard there.[93] John saw it as an inmate on Patmos, and the Lord told him to write what he saw.[94] The last two chapters of Revelation always fill me with joy. It's one of my secret weapons against depression and discouragement.

The angel tells John he wants to show him the bride, the wife of the Lamb.[95] We know who the Lamb of God is because that is what John the Baptist called Jesus.[96] John the Baptist also identified believers as the bride of Jesus.[97] *We* are his bride, his most beloved. The garden of New Jerusalem is the setting for a wedding, the wedding of Jesus Messiah, God's only begotten son, to us. All this time we have given our hearts to him, we have turned away from all other loves, we have waited for him, and now he has snatched us away from this life of poverty and tears and clothed us in white—not the white smock of servants but with a magnificent embroidered wedding gown.[98] As in any wedding, the bride is the center of attention, the groom's glory.

This holy city "comes down out of heaven from God."[99] It shines with the glory of God; its brilliance is like that of a very precious jewel, polished like jasper but clear as crystal. "It had a great high wall with twelve gates, and twelve angels at the gates."[100] Understand that angels in the Bible are nothing like angels you see on greeting cards. The angel in 2 Samuel 24:15–16 killed seventy thousand people in a couple of days. The angels in Revelation chapter 8 destroy the earth's ecosystems wholesale. All that effort by people to save the environment literally goes up in smoke. How about the angel in Revelation 10:1–2 who plants one foot on the land and one foot on the sea? When he speaks, it sounds like seven thunders. My point is that the holy city is a real paradise (walled garden), complete with the high wall, gates, and powerful guards.

Next, he tells us how big the city is: 12,000 stadia on a side and 12,000 stadia tall.[101] A *stadion (στάδιον)* was the Greek unit of measurement for the length of a stadium, which was about 185 meters, so this city is really big (12,000 x .185 km = 2,220 km on a side). At 1.6 km/mile that works out to 1,375 miles on a side. We are talking about a city with a footprint the size of India, but tall enough to have a thousand Indias stacked within it, each over a mile in height. The walls are 144 cubits thick. At two cubits to a yard, they are 72 yards thick; the twelve gates would have to be more like tunnels. Three to a side would put them over 450 miles apart.

So here is the way I picture it: the wedding feast begins, and here comes the bride, this huge beautiful city shining like a diamond, coming down from heaven; and the people who live there are you and me, all who have been made clean by the blood of Jesus and have been sealed his by the Spirit. It goes without saying that Paradise can't land on earth anywhere. If something as big as that were to land on the earth, it would probably destroy both. More than likely, it will just hang in orbit over the earth, and those who come and go from there will have to fly. People living down on the surface will look up and they will see our garden home. "The nations will walk by its light, and the kings of the earth will bring their splendor into it."[102]

As in the other gardens, John sees a fountain of pure water, the river of life, flowing out of the throne of God.[103] God the Father might be invisible,[104] but we will certainly see Jesus sitting there on the throne, who is his perfect image and likeness.[105] On each side of the river of life is a row of trees, the tree of life. We will both drink the water of life and eat the fruit of the tree of life. The trees will bear twelve different kinds of fruit, one every month.[106] The leaves of the trees will be sent down to heal the nations. The river of water in Paradise is a great deal like another from the Old Testament.

PHOTO BY: RICHARD RIVES – WWW.WYATTMUSEUM.COM

Out in the Arabian Desert, there stands a huge rock five stories tall. It looks as though it was split in two from the top with the precision of a laser. The cleft is plumb vertical and of even width. At the bottom of the cleft, there is a small chamber that bears the marks of water passing through it with tremendous force, carving smooth channels into the rock on either side of the cleft. The chamber has no crack or hole in the bottom. Wherever the water came from that carved into the rock, it had to come from above, not from below. I have a photograph of the rock and a close-up of the chamber in my study. After the children of Israel crossed over the Red Sea from Egypt into Arabia, they traveled into this desert until they ran out of water. God told Moses to strike the rock with his staff; and when he did, water gushed out.[107] Not just a little water either. Based on the size of the opening in the rock, it had to have been as much water as flows down a river the size of the Jordan. It gushed out in both directions from the cleft in the rock. It emanated from the cloud of God's presence that rested on top of the rock.[108] It was not natural water from the air or from springs in the earth; it was *living water* that flowed spontaneously from the presence of God. Paul refers to it this way: "They all ate the same spiritual food [the manna from heaven] and drank the same spiritual drink, for they drank from the spiritual rock that accompanied them, and that rock was Christ."[109] Paul is not saying that the huge rock moved along with them in the desert. He is saying that the water came forth from our *spiritual rock* who is Christ. Today, the rock still stands there; but without Christ, it is as dry as a bone. The river of life in Paradise flows from the person of Christ who sits on God's throne. It is living water.[110]

"And he that sat upon the throne said, 'Behold, I make all things new'" (Revelation 21:5, KJV)." He does not say he makes *all new things*.[111] The new earth and the new heavens will be filled with the things we have grown to love about this world except it will all be the way we always knew it should be: no more crying, no more death or grieving, no more pain of any kind.[112] Some people ask, "Will we just worship all the time forever?" I think not because throughout the Bible, there have always been set times for worship.[113] Some New Testament passages imply that we will also have administrative work to do because we will reign with him.[114] I hope Jesus lets me be one who gathers the leaves of his trees to take down to those who need healing. That's a job I would like.

Now I close with this prayer: Holy Father, in the mighty name of Jesus, send your spirit to fill my sister, your son's beloved bride, the one for whom he died, the one he covered and clothed in beautiful white, the one he has prepared a special place for in your lovely garden paradise. Amen.

STUDY QUESTIONS

Do you find courage when you spend time with God? Give examples.

_____

_____

When you think of God, how do you see him?

_____

_____

There are different ways to think about our place in the body of Christ:

Read Ephesians 4:12. What part of Christ's body are you?

_____

_____

Read 1 Corinthians 12:27–30. What are your gifts?

_____

_____

Review Revelation chapters 2–3. Which of the seven churches do you fit into? Why?

_____

_____

How easy is it for you to condemn parts of Christ's body (or church) that are different from you while excusing the parts of the body you agree with?

_____

_____

Review Revelation 1:20. How many of the stars or "angels" (pastors) of the seven churches did Jesus hold in his right hand? How many in his left? What does this mean to you?

_____

_____

Lot's wife disobeyed the angel's warning to not look back. Read Revelation 1:3. Is there a warning in there for us?

_____

_____

Revelation was written to provide hope and encouragement in a time of persecution against Christian believers. Believers are supposed to look forward to the end of the world as the beginning of a new age in which Christ will set everything right that is wrong on earth. Are you able to forgive those who have wronged you, knowing that they will ultimately face God's judgment? Please write why.

_____

_____

The robber on the cross next to Jesus was saved because he confessed his sin and asked Jesus to remember (or have mercy on) him. Read Matthew 17:20–21. How much faith do you need? Do you think you have that much?

_____

_____

LETTER FIVE

The Garden Tomb

My dear friend in Jesus,

While I was going over the preceding letters, I heard a sermon on the radio about the paramount place the resurrection of Jesus has for us. It is the final proof that Jesus is who he said he is: the promised Messiah of Israel, the Son of God. As God's Son, he was not like fallen men and women who are powerless to avoid sin and death. He was the only person who ever lived his life without any sin.[115] He also demonstrated by his resurrection that he has power over death, a power that only God has. Make no mistake: without the resurrection, Jesus's promises and claims would be as empty and ridiculous as those of the last political candidate you voted for. Jesus said he was one with the Father,[116] and then he proved it by voluntarily laying down his life and taking it up again.[117] That's when I realized that I almost forgot the most important garden in this amazing story of God's love for us: the garden tomb.

Father, in Jesus's name, help me gather my thoughts about this garden in a way that brings you glory. They are like the wind, going every which way. Let your Holy Spirit direct them so that your words go and do what you sent them for.[118] Amen.

This part of the story has a lot of witnesses, a number of women in particular. The death and resurrection of Jesus is set up in the Bible much like the testimony for a trial. Why might this be? Well, if the enemy wanted to get people to ignore the Bible and forget about the God revealed in it, it would make sense to debunk the claim that Jesus was actually dead and that he really did come back to life. Since everything in the Old Testament points forward to Christ and the New Testament reveals, by his resurrection, that Jesus is the Christ, an argument disproving the resurrection would wipe out the historical credibility of the whole Bible in one sweeping blow.

THE WRITERS

With the kind of foresight only God has, he provided us with four independent accounts that agree on all important points without being copies of each other. I'd like to begin with who the writers of these accounts were.

MATTHEW

This name means "Gift of Yahweh" but he is called Levi in Mark and Luke. We don't know whether Jesus renamed him Matthew like he did Simon Peter or if he was known as Matthew the Levite. He was a tax collector (or *publican*) and just walked off his job to follow Jesus.[119] Publicans were hated by Jews at least as much as the Internal Revenue Service is hated in our country. The difference was that tax collectors then weren't government employees; they bid on the right to collect taxes in a certain area as a business. Matthew was at the receipt of custom in Galilee, which would mean he collected import taxes for King Herod from people traveling on the highway. Whatever a publican could extort from people above the legally required amount was their sole source of income. Your ordinary Jew thought they were traitors to their nation and should be killed, so Matthew probably did not have many friends except for other publicans. Jesus took for apostles a number of men who would not have been approved by a search committee. One of the requirements of a publican's job was to be able to take shorthand. Since Matthew was present at the Sermon on the Mount, he was probably able to take it down verbatim. Matthew was an eyewitness to Jesus's entire public ministry.

Some writers compare the four Gospels to the four faces of the living creatures at the throne of God: the first a lion, the second an ox, the third a man, and the fourth an eagle.[120] Altar editions of the four gospels often have these pictured on the cover. The idea is that our Lord has four different aspects that deserve our adoration, and each gospel emphasizes a different one. Matthew presents Jesus as the Lion of the tribe of Judah[121] or the promised Messiah of the Jews. He writes in a way that assumes the reader is familiar with Jewish scripture and focuses on the words and sermons of Jesus more than the other writers do.

MARK

Marcus (Latin for "sledgehammer") was the Roman surname he adopted for his ministry. His Jewish name was John. He was called either Mark or John Mark to prevent confusion with the other John. Mark was a young man when he started following

Jesus. His mother, Mary, was probably a widow and had a large enough house in Jerusalem that it became a natural meeting place for the apostles and the early church. Peter went there when the angel let him out of prison while he was on death row,[122] and it was likely the house where the Holy Spirit was poured out on the believers on the day of Pentecost in Acts chapter 2. Mark was related to Barnabus (probably a cousin), and since Barnabus was a Levite, Mark would have been one too.[123] If you were a Levite in Israel, it meant your family did not get an inheritance of land but you were in the priestly tribe and were responsible for taking care of the temple and doing the work there. They were supported by the tithing of the people and the temple tax. Levites sometimes acted as local justices of the peace. They had to know how to read and write and were the traditional experts in Jewish law, so Mark would have gone to school. Barnabus and Mark both accompanied Paul during his first missionary journey.[124] At one point, Mark turned back; after that Paul refused to take him on the second missionary journey. Barnabus stood up for his cousin, and he and Paul parted ways over it; Barnabus took Mark one way, and Paul took Silas the other way.[125] Paul later reconciled with Mark and said he was very helpful to him.[126]

Peter authored two general letters to the church; but since he was not an educated man, Silas and Mark wrote for him. He even calls Mark his "son."[127] Mark was not an apostle, but he was with them in the garden of Gethsemane when Jesus was arrested.[128] He was a reliable eyewitness to Jesus's ministry in the city of Jerusalem (including his death and resurrection) and probably got the rest of his information from Peter. Some commentators go so far as to say that Mark's book is the gospel of Peter as penned by Mark.

This gospel presents Jesus as the ox, or the lowly servant of God. The other three gospels give a genealogy of Jesus, but no one cares what the pedigree of a servant is and Mark does not give one. Mark often explains Jewish idioms or translates the Aramaic or Greek word into Latin for his readers. It is clear that he was writing for the benefit of a Roman audience, those among whom he ministered with Paul and Barnabus. In proper Roman style he keeps his narrative brief, moves quickly from scene to scene, and focuses on the actions of Jesus, not his words. He uses the historical present tense to make his narrative more like a movie script and records more of the miracles of Jesus than any of the other gospel writers.

LUKE

Lukas was probably from Antioch in northern Syria and appears to be the only Gentile (non-Jewish) writer in the New Testament. He was trained as a physician, and became a traveling companion and a dear friend to Paul.[129] Due to his work as a doctor, he provides more detail to the healing miracles of Jesus and the apostles. He presents his gospel as an historical narrative in a manner that is easy to understand for a Western audience, translating some words into Greek. Luke wrote two books, his gospel as part one, and the book of Acts as part two. He joined Paul on his second missionary journey but stayed in Philippi (Greece) until Paul came back through on the way back from his third missionary journey.[130] He and Mark also traveled with Paul to Rome and stayed with him until Paul was tried and executed.[131] In his introductory comments, he explains that he drew from the oral testimony of the eyewitnesses and servants of Jesus and he also carefully investigated "everything from the beginning" (Luke 1:1–4). Luke could have interviewed Mary when they passed through

Ephesus and gives an account of the birth of Jesus with details only Mary would have known.

Luke's gospel shows Jesus as the Son of Man, emphasizing his humanity and feelings. More than the other gospels, Luke writes about Jesus's caring heart for the sick, the poor, outcasts, and toward women and children. His audience appears to have been readers of Greek who would be well-educated and Gentile, as he was. He is the one who chronicles the taking of the gospel beyond Israel to Gentiles by Paul and others.

JOHN

This name means "God is Grace." John the son of Zebedee is the fourth gospel writer. He never mentions his own name in his narratives but calls himself "the apostle whom Jesus loved" or "the other apostle." For this reason, he is called John the beloved. Jesus called John and his brother, James, the "sons of thunder" when they went to a Samaritan town and no one wanted to give Jesus a place to stay. They asked Jesus if they could call down fire from heaven on that town.[132] Jesus used this name for them as a gentle reminder that he came not to condemn but to save the world.[133] John was one of the three apostles who formed the inner circle of Jesus, who witnessed his transfiguration on the mountain,[134] and who went further into the garden of Gethsemane while Jesus struggled under the weight of our sin.[135] He rested his head on Jesus's breast at the Last Supper and, was able to hear it when Jesus said he was going to dip bread in the sauce and hand it to his traitor.[136] He was the first to recognize Jesus when he appeared on the beach after his resurrection.[137] John and James came from a family that owned fishing boats and employed fishermen. Peter was either their father Zebedee's partner or employee.

Some sources say that "Zebedee and Sons" was contracted to supply fish for the high priest's palace in Jerusalem. All we know from the Bible is that John was well enough known to the household of the high priest that he was admitted through the locked gate when Jesus was taken there for an illegal hearing on the night before he died.[138] John and James would have had the advantage of a good education since their father was well off and could afford private school. Zebedee allowed their mother, Salome, to give substantial financial help to Jesus and the apostles for their needs. John's grasp of Jewish idioms and symbolism is very deep. Many feel that he was the mystic in the group because of this. Like a bookend to Moses, who wrote the first five books of the Old Testament, John wrote the five last (in date) New Testament books: the gospel of John, three letters to the church, and the Revelation. We owe the Revelation to the fact that he wrote while he was in prison on the island of Patmos.[139] Patmos was like the infamous Alcatraz Island penitentiary in San Francisco Bay before they closed it. Fortunately, John outlived the governor who sentenced him and was released upon his death. He was younger than the other apostles and, according to church tradition, outlived all of them to a ripe old age.

John's gospel presents Jesus as the transcendent, all-seeing eagle, the Son of God. He appears to have the church in mind as his primary audience. He makes no attempt to write a chronological narrative but instead focuses on specific teachings and incidents from the life of Jesus to show who he was in his God nature as the I AM (Hebrew) or the Word (the Greek equivalent).[140] He was with Peter at the garden tomb.

THE WITNESSES

Next, I want to go over the witness list. Each of the four gospel writers lists who the witnesses were of Jesus's death, burial, and resurrection. Let's start with the witnesses to his death on the cross.

AT THE CROSS

- Four Roman soldiers who divided Jesus's clothing and threw dice to see who would get his undergarment.[141]

- The centurion, the officer in charge who declared that Jesus was truly the Son of God after the sun went dark and there was an earthquake during the crucifixion.[142]

- Simon from Cyrene in North Africa, father of Alexander and Rufus, a visitor for the high holy days who was pressed into service to carry Jesus's cross for him.[143] Tradition says Jesus collapsed while carrying his cross because of exhaustion. He had been whipped almost to death before Pilate earlier that day in a failed ploy to satisfy the Jews and release him.[144] After this, the soldiers took him to the barracks, put a bag over his head, and taunted him as they beat him in the face repeatedly.[145] Isaiah prophesied that Messiah would be "lifted up" (or crucified) and his appearance and form would be so disfigured that he would no longer have human likeness.[146] Perhaps this was why his disciples did not even recognize him when he was resurrected until after he showed his hands.[147]

- Wailing women from Jerusalem to whom Jesus predicts the impending fall of Jerusalem in 70 AD.[148]

- Two robbers who were crucified on Jesus's right and left; one goes to Paradise, the other presumably to hell.[149]

- The Jews: the gospel writers mention chief priests, rulers, teachers of the law (or scribes), and elders of the people who have come to watch, mock, and gloat.

- Mary, the mother of Jesus. Who can imagine her pain?

- John, the beloved apostle, whom Jesus commands to take charge of Mary.[150]

- Women of Galilee watching from a distance:

  - Mary of Magdala, listed first by all four writers

  - Mary the mother of James (the younger apostle) and Joses, wife of Alphaeus[151]

  - Mary, wife of Cleopas

  - Salome, Zebedee's wife, the mother of James (the older apostle) and John

  - "Many other" Galilean women who followed Jesus and were there for the holy days.

- The priests doing service in the temple witnessed the heavy curtain or veil of the temple being torn in two from top to bottom at the precise moment of Jesus's death.[152] Jesus's death eliminated the curtain of separation between God and his new temple, the church.[153] Animal sacrifices were no longer necessary to approach God.[154]

- Joseph from Arimathea, a prominent member of the Sanhedrin Council (Jewish legislature) who was secretly a disciple. Tradition holds that he owned ships that sailed the two-year trip to and from either Spain or Briton (Tarshish) to buy tin at the furthest frontier of the Roman Empire. He was not just rich but was one of the wealthiest men in the world. He comes boldly out of the closet and asks Pilate for the body of Jesus.[155] He and Nicodemus wrap the body and quickly put him in Joseph's own new tomb because after sunset, it is unlawful for them to do any work (it is the Sabbath). He rolls the heavy disk of stone in front of the entrance to the tomb.

- Nicodemus, another member of the Sanhedrin Council who came to Jesus by night to ask him questions. The most quoted verse in the New Testament was said during this conversation; and in it, Jesus predicted his crucifixion.[156] He buys about a hundred pounds of myrrh and aloe for embalming the body of Jesus and gives it to the Galilean women to prepare. He helps Joseph wrap the body and hurriedly put it into the garden tomb before the Jewish Sabbath at sunset.

- Pilate, the governor, is not present to witness the death of Jesus but asks the centurion to certify that he is dead before releasing the body to Joseph of Arimathea. The soldiers broke the legs of the two robbers (killing them) so they could be taken down before the Jewish Sabbath began to appease the Jews because it was Passover, the biggest Jewish holiday of the year. Jesus was already dead, so one of the soldiers put a spear into his left side (into his lung and heart) to make sure. Blood and water gushed out, indicating that he probably died of congestive heart failure (a broken heart) because his heart and lungs were full of fluid. He was really and truly dead, not just in a coma for three days, as some say.

WITNESSES TO THE BURIAL

- Joseph of Arimathea, mentioned above.

- Nicodemus, who helped him.

- Mary of Magdala, who watches from opposite the tomb. Magdala was one of the towns on the Sea of Galilee. She was among the women who followed Jesus and the apostles to care for their financial and domestic needs. Luke said that seven demons went out of her[157] but did not say who cast them out. We can only surmise that it was Jesus from her devotion to him afterward.

- "The other Mary" or "Mary, the mother of Joses" was with her. They take the spices and perfumes that Nicodemus bought and prepare them for embalming the body (the myrrh must be crushed and the aloe melted), but they have to wait for the Sabbath to be over before they can do the work because of Jewish law.

- Early the next morning (on the special Sabbath), the chief priests and Pharisees go to Pilate to say that Jesus predicted his resurrection after three days. So they *were* paying attention to what he said, even when Jesus's own disciples had forgotten that! They ask Pilate for a Roman watch to seal the tomb and make sure the disciples would not steal the body and claim that Jesus was alive again.

- Pilate is sick of this. They forced him to crucify a man he knew was innocent, his centurion and the believing Jews think he has killed God's son, and now they want a detachment of guards to watch the tomb. Even his wife warned him not to get involved.[158] He gives them his seal and a watch (four shifts of four soldiers) to guard the tomb, but you have to wonder what he is thinking when he tells them "Go, make the tomb as secure as you can."[159] Not long after this, he put down a rebellion in Samaria so brutally that when word got to the new emperor, it cost him his career. Historians say he returned to Europe to answer to the emperor and then took his own life, the customary act of a disgraced official.

GOLGOTHA AND INDIANA JONES

PHOTO BY DR. CARL RASMUSSEN – HOLYLANDPHOTOS.ORG

The place of crucifixion, *Gûlgaltá,* is Aramaic for "skull." The name appears in all of the gospels except Dr. Luke's, which uses *Kranion* or "cranium." Only one hill in the area has the likeness of a skull on it when the shadows are just right. On top of this, researchers have found square sockets cut into the stone of the same size as timbers used for crucifixion. The place was near a busy road into the city outside the north wall at the Damascus gate, just where you would want it if you believed that capital punishment is a deterrent for crime.

Hang on; this is about to get weird, but I'm not making it up. One socket has a crack through it that goes clear through the rock, believed to have been caused by an earthquake. Immediately beneath, there is a cavern called Jeremiah's grotto. It was part of Solomon's stone quarry, some of which was later converted into tombs. Since Jeremiah was taken captive to Egypt and stoned there,[160] his tomb in Jerusalem should be empty, but investigators insist that it has an occupant. There is enough evidence to suggest that a stone box containing the Ark of the Covenant could have been hidden there during the seventh or sixth century BC; the box is the right size and was carefully covered with skins and timbers, and then the chamber was tightly packed with rocks and the door was bricked closed. Excavating there is heavily regulated, but Ron Wyatt got permission and went in. He saw that the lid of the box was broken directly below the cracked socket.[161] He used a proctoscope to see into the box and saw some kind of furniture with pomegranates decorating the edges. Wyatt believed that when the spear was put into Jesus's side and blood and water gushed out, it could have run down the cross, through the crack in the socket, onto the cracked lid of the stone box below, and then onto the mercy seat, just as the high priest was required on the Day of Atonement (*Yom Kippur*) to sprinkle the blood of the sin offering onto it.[162]

CAN'T COUNT TO THREE

Something that always bothered me when I was younger was that Jesus supposedly died on Good Friday, spent "three days and three nights" in the tomb,[163] and then rose from the dead early on Sunday morning. Let me see … Jesus dies at 3:00 p.m. on a Friday. Saturday, Sunday, Monday. Easter, or resurrection day, should happen on Monday evening or maybe Tuesday morning if you do the math.

We aren't Jewish, so we have obviously missed something. First, we are used to our days beginning and ending at midnight, but the Jews recon the day from sunset to sunset. Secondly, there is the whole matter of what a Sabbath is. There are fifty-two Saturdays in a year, but the Jewish calendar has seventy Sabbaths. We still have to account for eighteen Sabbaths that aren't connected to the day of the week. Every twenty-eight days, there is a new moon (thirteen per year), which according to several passages in the Old Testament, were feast days or special Sabbaths.[164] That still leaves five more special Sabbaths for the high holy days specified in the law. During the week of Passover there are three: Passover happens on the fourteenth of Nisan on the Jewish lunar calendar (in March or April), the Feast of Unleavened Bread happens on the fifteenth of Nisan, and the Feast of First-Fruits happens on the sixteenth of Nisan. This is why John says they wanted to take the bodies down, because sunset was the start of the Sabbath that was a "high day"[165] or special Sabbath. It was not a Friday at all; otherwise it would have been an *ordinary* Sabbath. We can rely on the gospel accounts that Jesus was seen alive early on the morning on the first day of the week (Sunday) after at least three days and three nights in the tomb because during Passover week, you have three special Sabbaths in a row in addition to the normal Saturday Sabbath. That made it impossible for the women to wait just one day and then return with the spices and perfumes. Count to three backward from Sunday morning or, to be more exact, back from sunset on Saturday . . . Friday, Thursday, Wednesday. We should really celebrate Good Wednesday; it is the day he had to die to fulfill all the recorded facts. Thursday was a high day, so Joseph and Nicodemus had to hurry to comply with the law requiring the burial of a hanged person before sunset.[166] The days are still relatively short in March; and they had to get an audience with Pilate, get the linen cloths, buy the spices, go back to the cross, take the body down, wrap it, and put it somewhere safe all between "the ninth hour" (3:00 p.m.) and sunset on Wednesday.

THE GARDEN TOMB

The garden tomb where it is believed Jesus was buried is about 550 yards away from Golgotha as the crow flies, maybe a quarter of a mile at the most with the way the streets are. The Bible says that Joseph of Arimathea had a new tomb there in which no one had ever been laid. It was the sort of a tomb that only the very wealthy can afford,[167] with two interior rooms and a private walled garden in front of it. They were out of time, and the tomb was nearby. This was a practical decision, not a sentimental one; but there it is, another walled garden with a strong door (and guards) in this fantastic drama of God's love for us.

Along the ground in front of the opening was a gently sloped track on which rested a huge stone disk that leaned slightly into the block wall. With the slope of the track, it would be relatively easy to roll the stone down to cover the tomb's opening but much harder to roll it back open. We know this tomb had a garden because of what it says in John 19:41 and 20:15. It is the moment in the story to which all history looks either forward or back: *Mary mistook Jesus for the gardener.*

Mary of Magdala and Mary, the mother of Joses, return early Sunday morning with the myrrh-and-aloe preparation after waiting more than three days and three nights. Mark says they wonder how they will move the heavy stone so they can go in.[168] Based on this conversation, I have to guess that they are unaware that Pilate has sealed the tomb and posted a military watch there. Otherwise, they would be wondering how they will get past the guards. Fortunately for them, they will not have to do a thing about either problem.

Each gospel writer tells the story from the viewpoint of different witnesses who saw different things at different times, so we will have to carefully piece together the accounts to get the whole story. Here is the rundown on who saw what:

- Matthew says the two Marys witnessed a violent earthquake, "for an angel of the Lord came down from heaven and, going to the tomb, rolled back the stone and sat on it.... The guards were so afraid of him that they shook and became like dead men." The angel tells them that Jesus is no longer in the tomb since he has risen (as he said he would), and invites them to look inside for themselves. The angel commands them to go tell the disciples Jesus has risen from the dead and will meet them in Galilee.[169] They turn to leave the tomb and see Jesus there. For the rest of that conversation we will have to go to John. Matthew writes that as the women were heading back to the house where the apostles were staying, the guards at the tomb recovered and some of them went to the chief priests to report. This seems highly irregular, as if they had been bribed by the priests to report only to them if something happened. I am speculating, but it seems that they would have reported to the centurion and Pilate if they were reporting up the chain of command. The chief priests were aware that the centurion believed in Jesus, and they knew Pilate would love nothing more than to discredit them. My guess is that the chief priests were worried enough that Jesus would really come back alive that they did this to hedge their bets. They quickly meet with the elders of the Jews and come up with a spin control plan. They give the guards a large sum of money (or bribe) and tell them to say they fell asleep, and while they were sleeping some of Jesus's disciples came and stole the body. The penalty for falling asleep on watch in the Roman army was death; part of their duty was to keep each other awake. The chief priests tell them that if word comes to the governor's ears, they will intervene.[170]

How could the disciples roll the big stone out of the way without waking four guards? How could the guards know who came to steal the body if they were sleeping that soundly? Did anyone wonder how they slept right through a violent earthquake? And why would the disciples unwrap the body and leave the linens neatly folded if they were stealing it under the noses of sleeping guards? If the guards wakened to see who was stealing the body, why didn't they arrest and detain them? The story just does not work unless you can bribe everyone that asks too many questions. Did the chief priests know that Jesus had risen from the dead? I think we have to say yes, they did. Did they know he was in fact the Messiah of Israel? Again, I say yes, they had to know it by this time, and they were willing to pay a large sum of money to keep it quiet. Their intervention ended up proving the very thing they hoped to discredit.

- Mark adds that Salome was with Mary Magdalene and the other Mary. In his version, the tomb is already open when they get there. If Mark's source was Salome and she came along a little after the others, his version makes sense. By the time she arrives, the earthquake has passed and the heavy stone has been rolled aside. Now, Mark reports that the angel is inside the empty tomb where he has been showing it to the two Marys. He adds this detail: "But go, tell his disciples *and Peter*, 'He is going ahead of you into Galilee. There you will see him, just as he told you'" (Mark 16:7). The angel wanted to make sure Peter knew he was still invited to come meet Jesus after he had denied him at the high priest's house. I imagine up to this point, Peter is having about the worst day in his life. Judas, his brother apostle, betrayed Jesus and had gone out and hung himself.[171] Jesus was given a mock trial and executed, and now this. Peter knows he also betrayed Jesus, and maybe suicide has privately crossed his mind too. Next, Mark inserts that Mary Magdalene was the first to see the resurrected Lord, but he does not place it in the sequence of events or provide any additional details of the meeting.

• Luke's version follows Mark's with the door being open, but indicates that there were two angels inside the open tomb. Luke says the witnesses were Mary Magdalene; Joanna; Mary, the mother of James (and Joses); and the others with them who went to tell the apostles about the empty tomb. Luke appears to be in contradiction to Matthew and Mark on the question of one vs. two angels, but John's version sets this straight since he says Mary Magdalene came to the tomb before *and after* the apostles did. Luke must have had sources that were there both times as he has blended together details from both visits as though it all happened at once. These two angels were inside the tomb later in the day, after the guards were gone and the apostles had come and gone. Mark and Luke do not even mention the guards because by the time their sources arrived at the scene, they were gone.

• John reports that Mary Magdalene went to the tomb early on Sunday morning, while it was still dark.[172] She saw the stone rolled back so ran to tell Peter and John ("the other apostle"). She says, "They have taken the Lord out of the tomb and *we* don't know where they have put him!" She is speaking for the other Mary as well as for herself; they saw the empty tomb before anyone else did, with Salome only a little behind them. John and Peter both run to see, but John outruns Peter and gets there first. He stands at the door, peering in, but waits there. Peter catches up and goes in with John following. This time, there is no mention of angels. The angel that opened the door is gone, and the two that will be seen inside have not come yet. Both of them see the linen strips lying there, and John mentions that the burial cloth that had been around Jesus's head was folded and lying by itself. They leave to tell the others; but apparently, Mary Magdalene has followed them back to the tomb the second time and stays there after they go, crying. John does not mention the other women; but from Luke's account, we know they came also. This has to be when they see two angels inside the tomb. We know they leave before Mary because they miss seeing Jesus. Mary bends down to look into the tomb again, and she sees the two angels sitting inside, where the body had been, one at the head and the other at the foot. They ask her why she is crying, and she tells them what she told

Peter and John, that someone has taken her Lord away and she does not know where they have put him. She turns around to go and sees Jesus standing there. He is risen from the dead but is not yet glorified. For some reason, Mary doesn't recognize him. Were there tears in her eyes? Was she looking down? Was his face hidden? Was he so scarred and disfigured that Isaiah's prophesy had come true; he did not look like the man he was anymore?[173] We just don't know. Jesus says, "Woman, why are you crying? Who is it you are looking for?" This is the same question he asked the high priest's servant when he came to Gethsemane to arrest him.[174] It is the same question he asks each of us in one way or another: "Who do people say the Son of Man is? Who do you say I am?"[175] John said she thought he was the gardener. Jesus says, "Mary," and then she knows him.

If this were a musical, this scene would reprise the Song of Songs. Mary clings to Jesus and will not let him go. She rose from her bed while it was still dark to search the city for the shepherd she loves. It is eerie how the passage in the Song even foretells the presence of the angel watchmen at the tomb:

> All night long on my bed I looked for the one my heart loves; I looked for him but did not find him. I will get up now and go about the city, through its streets and squares; I will search for the one my heart loves. So I looked for him but did not find him. The watchmen found me as they made their rounds in the city. "Have you seen the one my heart loves?" Scarcely had I passed them when I found the one my heart loves. I held him and would not let him go ...
>
> Song 3:1–4

Mary Magdalene is every one of us. How like Jesus to appear as the gardener! Are we not his garden? Somehow, amid all the running back and forth of the Galilean women and the apostles between the places where they were staying in Jerusalem and the tomb outside the Damascus gate, Jesus catches Mary for an intimate moment alone, there in the walled garden, to reveal himself as the Gardener of her heart. Whatever else happens after this, Mary knows that Jesus is *her* Lord, and no one will be able to convince her otherwise or pull her away from him. She is "a garden locked up, a spring enclosed, a sealed fountain."[176]

STUDY QUESTIONS

Read 2 Corinthians 5:10. We also will stand trial; not for our sins or for salvation but to receive the due reward for what we have done with the new life he gave us. Does this make you feel happy or fearful? Why?

_____

_____

Why do you think Jesus chose the people he did to be apostles? Do you wonder why he chose you?

_____

_____

Does it help you relate better to Jesus knowing that he was fully human and felt the same things we do? Why or why not?

_____

_____

Jesus called John and James the "sons of thunder" as a gentle rebuke for wanting to destroy the people for their inhospitable behavior.

Has he ever had to discipline you for an attitude you had? Explain.

_____

_____

If he were to give you a nickname, what do you think it would be?

_____

_____

Read Mark 16:7. Jesus forgave Peter after he denied him three times. Do you think it still troubled Peter for the rest of his life? What about your sins? Have you confessed them and asked Jesus to forgive you? If you have, do they continue to trouble you even though you are forgiven?

_____

_____

In this garden, Jesus appears as the gardener. Have you ever met a person and wondered if it was Jesus in disguise? Give an example.

_____

_____

LETTER SIX

The Garden of My Heart

My dear friend in Jesus,

In this last letter, it is my desire that you come with me into the private garden of my heart. The things I show you here are things that even those who know me well have not heard me speak about. Holy Father, I pray that by your Spirit we would be one in your son, Jesus Christ, as he is in you, and you are in him.[177]

When I was fifteen, my world ended. My father took a job in another state, and we moved away from all the people I knew and loved. When you are fifteen, your friends are your world. I stayed in the cult I belonged to, but I didn't know the new people and they didn't know me; it was all external. The program for teenagers there was under leaders who did not lead. They thought if we played unsupervised basketball every Wednesday while they sat and talked with each other it would somehow help us to form our lives. My heart was 1,250 miles away, where I used to live. I dove into my new school and my favorite avocation both then and now: music. I took lessons from the president of the International Clarinet Society and won several awards at state contests. I tried out to be the drum major for the marching band and got the job. I signed up to be in plays. I won a scholarship to study music in college. I was looking for anything that would make me feel alive again inside after the cataclysmic loss of everyone I cared about. Most of all, I missed the girl I thought I would marry someday, whom I had to leave behind. I think the reason I enjoy writing now is that for years, I wrote letters every day, love letters. During the time I spent writing letters, the dead feeling faded away and for a few minutes, I felt like I was home with my friends again. I never got into drugs. I had this.

As soon as school was out, I bought a bus ticket and went back to my hometown for two weeks, staying with friends. Things had changed a lot. My girl acted strange. My clique of friends had dispersed. My best friend had moved to another city to live with his dad. I went to the home of my old mentor from church and asked him to pray for me. He sat me in a chair, put his hands on my head, and started praying. After a few minutes, I could not hear his voice any longer; I was not in my body.

I know there are people who learn to meditate, who can leave their body at will. "Astral travel" they call it. At one time, I studied with some of them, but that is a story for another book. Let me just say I don't recommend it. This was different from that. I had never left my body before and did not know where I was. I had been snatched away from my ordinary consciousness by a power beyond my own. I started seeing and hearing things that might happen one day in the future, very frightening things: a voice speaking from heaven, an earthquake, tall buildings collapsing, the ground opening up and people falling in. God was judging the world, and it is not that far away in our future. I was in the middle of the street in a downtown district, and I died in the earthquake as the buildings fell. The Holy Spirit showed me two futures, and the choice was mine. This was my future if I did not follow Jesus. This death was bitter because I knew about God but went away from him.

Now I was not only out of my body but I was out of the body that left my body, *out of my mind,* if you want to put it that way. I was only spirit, and the Holy Spirit showed me my future in Christ. I was suddenly plunged into the most brilliant light, but it did not hurt my eyes or burn my skin. I could not see the sun; it was as if the light was everywhere, so nothing cast a shadow. I did not feel air moving against my skin. The absence of that seemed strange. I could not remember having died. I was alive in the body, and then I was here. The first thing I recognized was butterflies, and there were birds singing. I was standing in a garden, a huge field of wildflowers. Some distance away, I saw a hill, and on it there was a man wearing white, beckoning me to come up. As soon as I started moving, I was already there; I did not have to walk. When I drew near, I saw that it was Jesus. I can't tell you how I knew this. I just did. I did not have time to fall down before him. He quickly took me into a full embrace; and when he held me, the hole in my spirit was completely filled up and ran over. I never knew what love or intimacy was until this. I was made for him; we all were. We did not speak. There was nothing to say. I knew his heart and he knew mine without saying anything.

Now that my spirit was whole, Jesus took me by my shoulders and turned me around. When I turned, I saw below us the whole earth. I don't know how this is possible, but I saw all of it at once, not just the side facing us. My vision was so clear that I could look down and see everything down to the smallest detail. I saw past, present, and future all at the same time. We stood there on that garden hilltop for a long time, reviewing my life; and Jesus showed me all the things he did for me that I did not know before, the places where he helped me and the things he was able to accomplish through me when I did not even know he was doing something. He gave me the gift of perspective. He told my story the way he wrote it, not the way I saw it from my human experience. I didn't just feel peace and joy; I *possessed* them like a fountain of living water flowing out of my belly.[178] I had life that can't die again; I was resurrected from the deadness of my spirit to everlasting life.

Then I was in my body again, sitting on a chair, and my old mentor was still praying over me. This whole thing happened in the blink of an eye. I don't think it had that much to do with the man whose hands were on my head, but he was willing to be an instrument even if we did belong to a cult; and Jesus was willing to use him anyway, the way he is willing to use any of us if we will let him. I was in a cult, but I was also saved by Jesus, and I wasn't the only one there who was saved. I think there were a lot of us.

HUNGER AND THIRST

I have not thought about this vision for many years until just recently, when I had a strange dream that shook me to the core. In my dream, I moved about and interacted with people and the world, but the confusion inside my head was gone. My mind was suddenly quiet, a deafening silence after five decades of noise. *I felt what it would be like if I had the righteousness of Jesus.* I knew the right thing to do every moment. I did not have to spend any mental energy deciding what I should be doing, the best thing to say, the best use of my time and abilities; I just knew those things. I felt more helpful, more capable, and more effective than I ever have before. I knew that what I said and did was producing the maximum positive influence over people and events that I was capable of for the benefit of the kingdom of God. I felt fully realized.

But that wasn't all. I had the *right motivation* in my heart for doing the right thing. I never really thought about this before, so give me a moment to explain. I try to do the right thing. Sometimes I hit it. Sometimes I miss. But I really do try. What I realized in my dream is that even when I do the right thing, my motivation is self-interested. To be frank here, I have to admit that my motivation, my reasons, my payoff stinks to heaven even when my actions are good. I hope someone will notice me doing well. I hope they will think well of me for it. I hope it will bring me some sort of advantage or reward either now or in heaven. *I even need forgiveness when I do right.* I need grace no matter what I do.

Jesus did not do the right thing to be noticed or to win the approval of others. He deliberately did the right thing when he knew full well it would offend people and make him enemies. He did not do the right thing for a reward. He did the right thing because his father was working in him doing those things, he was moving in his father's perfect will.[179] When I do good things, I have to admit it isn't the truth about me; it's the truth about him.

To say it another way, when a sinner sins, he knows his heart is selfish. If he admits this to himself and to Jesus, and wants in his heart to change his ways, Jesus forgives him. He hungers and thirsts for righteousness. But the one who does right is just as evil and selfish in his heart as the sinner. Maybe you killed someone and now you are doing time for it, but what righteous person has not killed many times in his heart? If thoughts could kill, we'd all be murderers. So when the Pharisee hides behind his good works and does not think he needs forgiveness for anything, he is further away from God than the murderers, prostitutes, and drug dealers who recognize they are evil and hunger to be like the righteous. I never knew how offensive my inner self was to God,[180] not until I had this dream.

It was so vivid and real that I did not know I was dreaming until I started to wake up. I felt the righteousness of Jesus slipping away, my own crowded and conflicted mind returning. I wanted to shout "No!" I never knew what it meant before when Jesus said, "Blessed are those who hunger and thirst for righteousness,"[181] but I do now. I would give anything to have the righteousness of Jesus like I did in my dream. I have to trust that his righteousness is more than enough for me.

REVIVAL

All across America, pastors and churches are praying for revival. Since the Great Awakening of 1783 under the preaching of Jonathan Edwards, there have been approximately fifty-four revivals in thirty-five countries of a magnitude large enough to attract the attention of historians.[182] That averages out to a revival every 4.2 years. One of them happened right here in Spokane, Washington. John G. Lake was filled with the Holy Spirit at the Azusa Street Revival in 1907 in Los Angeles, and then he went to South Africa with Thomas Hezmalhalch to start the Pentecostal movement there where thousands were also filled. He later came to Spokane and opened offices called the Healing Rooms on the second floor of the Rookery Building, where he prayed over the sick. Between 1915 and 1920, his staff documented over a hundred thousand miraculous healings. It was a hard time to be in the hospital business here.

I have been to the rooms where John G. Lake worked. They were reopened by Cal Pierce in 1999, and I started going there with my wife for prayer that same year. Sometimes it was so crowded we just sat in the outer corridor with our backs to the wall where they were praying for people. We were close enough to the healing power of the Lord that we got what we came for right there. The first time we went, I was completely healed of a heart condition I had. I had a cardiologist, so my problem was documented. For years, when I took my pulse, every third beat skipped. I used to have to stop halfway up a long flight of stairs to let my heart slow down or I would feel faint. One day, at the hospital, I clocked my heart at 240 beats per minute just standing still. During the prayer, I did not feel anything happen; but when we went downstairs to the street level, I had this sudden urge to run. I ran around the entire block, and my heart was just fine. It has been ever since.

In many ways, the American church has become like the church at Laodicea in Revelation 3. Our focus is mostly on ourselves: our doctrine, our music, our building, our programs, our goals, our growth. We are busy doing good things, and we think that makes us okay. Revivals of the past have come among people who were broken before God, who were anything but okay with themselves. So why shouldn't there be a revival in America's correctional facilities? Why not among those who know their need? Why would Jesus not come among the publicans and sinners, the prostitutes and robbers today as he did before?

I have visited many kinds of churches, and I have been to church services in our local correctional facilities. To tell the truth, the inmates sing with more passion, as loud as they can. They pray with more fear of the Almighty. They don't come to watch; they *worship*. They know they fall short of what is taught in every way. They are broken before God, beggars at his feet, afraid to even look up. Inmates are the kind of people Jesus was talking about when he said, "Blessed are the poor in spirit."[183] Check out the word for "poor" in your lexicon, and it doesn't mean someone below the poverty line, barely making it. It means "utterly dependent, unable to earn anything." That's us. We are utterly dependent on God for his grace no matter what we do, no matter how good we become. We can't earn a thing.

I think it is time for revival in America, and the place where it could happen is in our correctional facilities. You can't pray in schools anymore, but you can in prison. You can't talk about God at the office anymore, but you can in prison. In some ways, inmates might be freer than the rest of us. Paul wrote great epistles from prison. John wrote the Revelation while imprisoned on Patmos. All the apostles were jailed at one time or another. Tradition says they were all executed except John. They weren't the only ones who paid that price for the love of Jesus inside of them.

Emperor Claudius II cancelled all engagements and marriages in Rome in 297–298 AD because he desperately needed more soldiers and he thought marriages were keeping the men from signing up. St. Valentine and St. Marius continued to perform marriages in secret. When Valentine was found out, he was beaten with clubs and Claudius sentenced him to death. While awaiting his sentence, he befriended the daughter of the jailer who brought his food to him, turning her to Jesus. On the night before he was executed, he wrote her a letter of love and encouragement, signing it, "Your Valentine." February 14, Valentine's Day, wasn't his birthday. It was the day his execution was carried out.

You never know if the small act of love you do for someone will become a day for the whole world to remember God's love. You don't know how many people your letters will save. You don't know whose heart is breaking when they see how much you care or whose worship became real for the first time because you were singing next to her. You *will* know though. When you meet Jesus in Paradise, there is a garden there with wildflowers, butterflies, and birds, where the light is so brilliant and diffuse that nothing casts a shadow. There is a place in that garden where you will see him alone and know him, the Gardener of your heart, and he will show you all these things.

Holy Father, in Jesus's precious name, send your Spirit with these letters to places where you are ready to give the gift of eternal life, and bring revival to all those who know you but lost their way. May I finally meet my dear friend in Jesus when we come to be with you forever.

STUDY QUESTIONS

(Please write about your heart garden.)

Have you ever felt like your life ended even though you were still alive? If your answer is yes, what made you feel this way?

_____

_____

The author mentioned that he studied for a time with people who knew how to leave their body at will and cautioned readers not to try it. Why do you think that could be dangerous?

_____

_____

Read 2 Corinthians 12:1–6.
In this letter, Paul recounts a vision in which he saw Paradise, but he does not want to tell it as though it happened to him. Why?

_____

_____

Why do you think very few people have visions like this?

_____

_____

What added responsibility or cost do you think a person who has a vision from God must bear? What did it cost Paul?

_____

_____

Do people think of Paul as a super saint because of his revelations? In light of what Paul said about his vision, is this view of him wrong or right?

_____

_____

How do _you_ know for sure that God is real and that paradise is waiting for you when you die?

_____

_____

Do you hunger and thirst for righteousness? Explain.

_____

_____

Why is it better to be a sinner and know it than to be a respectable person that feels no guilt?

_____

_____

If a revival were to break out where you live, what do you think would happen?

_____

_____

Does revival ever come to just one person? How would that look?

_____

_____

Even though he was not married himself, Saint Valentine paid for his support of biblical marriage with his life. Do Christians today believe in marriage that strongly? Why or why not?

_____

_____

Review Galatians 5:22–23.
What can you do in your current situation that might possibly affect the life of another person or turn them to Jesus?

_____

_____

Could you be making a difference in others without knowing it?

_____

_____

ENDNOTES

1   John 10:14–18, Hebrews 12:2

2   Genesis 2:5–6

3   Genesis 2:22–25

4   Ezekiel 28:13

5   Luke 23:43, 2 Corinthians 12:4, Revelation 2:7

6   Genesis 1:31

7   Genesis 3:5

8   Matthew 23:15

9   Genesis 50:20

10   1 Kings 3:10–13, 10:23; 2 Chronicles 1:11–12, 9:22

11   Song of Songs 1:6

12   Psalm 23:1, 80:1; John 10:11

13   Matthew 8:20, Luke 9:59

14   Song of Songs 1:9–11, 17

15   John 14:1–5

16   Song of Songs 3:6

17   Isaiah 63:1

18   Zechariah 12:10, 13:6, 14:4

19   Song 3:7–8

20   Song of Songs 4:1–9

21   Galatians 3:26, 4:1–7

22   Romans 8:1

23   John 17:26

24   Ephesians 4:30

25   Matthew 26:28

26   Exodus 28:33

27   Hebrews 3:1

28   1 Kings 7:18–20

29   1 Corinthians 3:16

30   Psalm 17:8

31   Revelation 7:14

32   John 10:28

33   Mark 14:3–5, John 12

34   John 14:27

35   Exodus 30:24–25

36   Leviticus 1:9

37   Romans 12:1

38   1 Corinthians 13:1–7

39   Numbers 16:35–40

40   Leviticus 16:13

41   Ephesians 6:16

42   Matthew 2:11

43   Exodus 30:23

44   New Testament Lexical Aids, supplemental material from the *Hebrew-Greek Key Study Bible* NIV, 1996 AMG International, Inc.

45   Matthew 16:24

46   Esther.2:12

47   Esther 4:11–16

48   John 19:39

49   Isaiah 53:5

50   Mark 15:23

51   1 Corinthians 15:55

52   John 19:39

53   Proverbs 3:13–14

54   2 Thessalonians 3:3

55   John 20:22

56   Acts 2:2

57   Mark 15:43–46

58   Matthew 26:36–40, Mark 14:32–37

59   Luke 22:43–44

60   John 15:13

61   Isaiah 53:6

62   2 Corinthians 5:21

63   Hebrews 12:2

64   Genesis 3:9

65   Genesis 3:21

66   Psalm 145:18–19, Romans 10:13

67   John 18:3–5

68   Exodus 3:13–14
69   Matthew 26:52–53
70   Mark 14:51
71   John 19:30
72   John 15:17
73   Revelation 3:9
74   Acts 4:34
75   Acts 2:42
76   Genesis 3:24
77   Numbers 22–25, 31:15
78   John 6:32–58
79   Genesis 10:8–10, chapter 11
80   1 Kings 16:31
81   Revelation 6:9–11
82   Revelation 3:20
83   1 Thessalonians 4:16–18
84   Luke 17:28–30
85   Genesis 11:27–28, 12:4
86   Genesis 13:10
87   Genesis 19:23–26
88   Matthew 13–24–30, 36–43
89   Matthew 13:47–50
90   Matthew 25:1–12
91   Luke 23:43
92   Acts 14:19
93   2 Corinthians 12:4
94   Revelation 1:19
95   Revelation 21:9
96   John 1:29
97   John 3:26–29
98   Psalm 45:14
99   Revelation 21:10
100   Revelation 21:12
101   Revelation 21:15–16
102   Revelation 21:24
103   Revelation 22:1
104   Colossians 1:15
105   Hebrews 1:3, John 14:9

106   Revelation 22:2
107   Exodus 17:5–6, Isaiah 48:21
108   Exodus 17:6
109   1 Corinthiens 10:3
110   Jeremiah 17:13
111   John Eldridge makes this point in his book, *Desire*.
112   Revelation 21:4
113   Job 1:6 suggests this is true in heaven also.
114   2 Timothy 2:12, Revelation 22:5
115   Hebrews 4:15
116   John 10:30
117   John 10:17–18
118   Isaiah 55:10–11
119   Matthew 9:9–11
120   Revelation 4:7, Ezekiel 1:10
121   Revelation 5:5
122   Acts 12:12
123   Colossians 4:10, Acts 4:36
124   Acts 12:25
125   Acts 15:36–39
126   2 Timothy 4:11
127   1 Peter 5:12–13
128   Mark 14:51
129   Colossians 4:14
130   Acts 20:6
131   Philemon 23
132   Mark 3:17, Luke 9:51–65
133   John 12:47
134   Matthew 17:1–2
135   Matthew 26:37
136   John 13:22–26
137   John 21:4:7
138   John 18:15
139   Revelation 1:9
140   John 20:30–31, 1:1
141   John 19:23–24
142   Matthew 27:50–54
143   Mark 15:21

144 John 19:1–6

145 Matthew 27:30, Mark 15:19

146 Isaiah 52:13–14

147 Luke 24:30–31

148 Luke 23:28–31

149 Luke 23:39–43

150 John 19:26–27

151 Luke 6:15

152 Matthew 27:51, Mark 15:38, Luke 23:45

153 1 Corinthians 3:16, 2 Corinthians 6:16

154 Hebrews 9; the entire chapter amplifies this.

155 John 19:38, Mark 15:43

156 John 3:14–16

157 Luke 8:2–3

158 Matthew 27:19

159 Matthew 27:65

160 Jeremiah 43:6–7. At least five ancient writers (Elmakin, Epiphanius, Abulpharagius, Jerome, and Tertullian), quoted by later historians, say that Jeremiah died in Egypt, that the Jews stoned him to death there, in a place called *Tahpanhes*.

161 Ron Wyatt, Discoveries; www.wyattmuseum.com; http://www.arkdiscovery.com/aoc-1.htm.

162 Leviticus 16:14–15

163 Matthew 12:40

164 Nehemiah 10:33 for example

165 John 19:31

166 Deuteronomy 21:22

167 Isaiah 53:9

168 Mark 15:3

169 Matthew 28:2–7

170 Matthew 28:14

171 Matthew 27:5

172 John 20:1

173 Isaiah 52:13–14

174 John 18:4

175 Matthew 16:13–15

176 Song of Songs 4:12

177   John 17:20–23
178   John 7:38
179   John 14:10
180   Jeremiah 17:9
181   Matthew 5:6
182   *500 Years of Revival History*, author unknown
183   Matthew 5:3